Reconciliation

We are your people, the sheep of your flock.

Program Director's Manual

ACKNOWLEDGMENTS

Scripture quotations contained herein are from the *New Revised Standard Version Bible: Catholic Edition,* copyright © 1989, 1993 Division of Christian Education of the National Council of the Churches of Christ in the United States of America. All rights reserved.

Excerpts from the Rite of Christian Initiation of Adults © 1985, International Committee on English in the Liturgy, Inc. (ICEL); excerpts from Pastoral Care of the Sick © 1982, ICEL; excerpts from the Rite of Penance © 1974 ICEL; excerpts from the Rite of Baptism for Children © 1969, ICEL. All rights reserved.

Excerpts from "Letter to Families from Pope John Paul II,"Pope John II, 3ʳᵈ printing, © 1994; "Misericordia Dei" (On Certain Aspects of the Celebration of the Sacrament of Penance, April 2002); "Novo Millennio Ineunte" (To the Bishops, Clergy, Lay Faithful at the Close of the Great Jubilee of the Year 2000); Daughters of St. Paul, Boston, MA.

Excerpts from "The Dogmatic Constitution on the Church," "The Pastoral Constitution on the Church in the Modern World from *Vatican Council II Volume 1, New Revised Edition: The Conciliar & Post Conciliar Documents* edited by Austin Flannery, O.P. copyright © 1998, Costello Publishing Company, Inc. Northport, NY is used by permission of the publisher, all rights reserved. No part of these excerpts may be reproduced, stored in a retrieval system, or transmitted in any form or by any means—electronic, mechanical, photocopying, recording or otherwise, without express permission of Costello Publishing Company.

Excerpts from the English translation of the *Catechism of the Catholic Church* for the United States of America copyright © 1994, United States Catholic Conference, Inc.—Libreria Editrice Vaticana. English translation of the *Catechism of the Catholic Church: Modifications from the Editio Typica,* copyright © 1997, United States Catholic Conference, Inc.—Libreria Editrice Vaticana.

Excerpts from *General Directory for Catechesis,* © 1997, Libreria Editrice Vaticana.

Excerpts from *Music in Catholic Worship* © 1983, United States Catholic Conference, Washington, D.C.

Excerpts from *The Canon Law Letter and Spirit* © The Canon Law Trust, 1995, The Liturgical Press, Collegeville, MN.

Cover Design by Kristy O. Howard

Cover Illustration by Karen Malzeke-McDonald

Nihil Obstat
Rev. Msgr. Glenn D. Gardner, JCD
Censor Librorum

Imprimatur
✝ Most Rev. Charles V. Grahmann
Bishop of Dallas

October 25, 2002

The Nihil Obstat and Imprimatur are official declarations that the material reviewed is free of doctrinal or moral error. No implication is contained therein that those granting the Nihil Obstat and Imprimatur agree with the contents, opinions, or statements expressed.

Send all inquiries to:
RCL • Resources for Christian Living
200 East Bethany Drive
Allen, Texas 75002-3804

Toll Free   877-275-4725
Fax   800-688-8356

Visit us at www.FaithFirst.com

Printed in the United States of America

20454   ISBN 0-7829-1024-6

1 2 3 4 5 6 7 8 9 10
03 04 05 06 07 08 09 10

Dedication

This program is dedicated to
Richard C. Leach
1927–2001
founder and continuing inspiration of RCL and recipient of the Pro Ecclesia et Pontifice Cross bestowed by Pope John Paul II in recognition of outstanding service to the Church.

SACRAMENT PREPARATION DEVELOPMENT TEAM

Developing a sacrament program requires the talents of many gifted people working together as a team. RCL is proud to acknowledge these dedicated people who contributed to the development of this sacrament preparation program.

Writing Team
Rev. Louis J. Cameli
Rev. Robert D. Duggan
Jacquie Jambor
Mary Beth Jambor
Diane Lampitt

Advisors
Rev. Louis J. Cameli
Theological Advisor

Rev. Robert D. Duggan
Liturgical Advisor

Elaine McCarron, SCN
Catechetical Advisor

Marina A. Herrera
Hispanic Consultant

Ed DeStefano
General Editor

Lisa Brent
Art and Design Director

Pat Bracken
Kristy O. Howard
Designers

Laura Fremder
Electronic Page Makeup

Jenna Nelson
Production Director

Patricia A. Classick
Ronald C. Lamping
Project Editors

Joseph Crisalli
Demere Henson
Web Site Producers

Maryann Nead
President/Publisher

Reconciliation
Program Director's Manual

Part One

For the
Program Director

About This Section

Part One: For the Program Director

This sacrament preparation program provides resources for the immediate preparation of candidates prior to the celebration of Reconciliation. Children and young people in this preparation would be considered catechized in the faith and participating in ongoing catechesis for their age group.

This sacrament preparation program is designed for:

Baptized children of catechetical age (seven years and older) who are now preparing for the sacrament of Reconciliation.

This section is designed to assist in the implementation of the program.

You will find many practical tools, "how-to's," and inspiring resources.

This section includes:

- **Welcome**
- **Models for Using the RCL Sacrament Preparation Program**
- **Program Philosophy**
- **Scope and Sequence**
- **Role of the Family, the Catechist, and the Assembly**
- **Initial Letter to Parents**
- **Guidelines for Planning the Celebration of the Sacraments**
  - **Rite for Reconciliation of Individual Penitents**
  - **Rite for Reconciliation of Several Penitents with Individual Confession and Absolution**

- **Professional Articles**

  These articles can be used to enrich your own background, catechist training, parent meetings, adult education, parish resources, parish/school staff development, pastoral council formation, liturgy committee updating, and for reprint in the parish bulletin or parish newsletter.

  - **Readiness for the Sacraments**
  - **Learning the History: The Essential Parts of the Sacrament**
  - **The Paths of Forgiveness: The Many Ways God's Forgiveness Touches Our Lives**
  - **An "Uninterrupted Task": Continuing Conversion and Conscience Formation**
  - **Sin and Grace**
  - **The Sacrament of Reconciliation: The Church's Practice and Understanding of the Sacrament**
  - **The Church as a Reconciled and Reconciling Community**
  - **Symbol and Ritual in the Preparation for Sacraments**

- Frequently Asked Questions
- Using the *Reconciliation* Music CD
- Using RCL's "Sacraments" Web Site
- Checklist for the Director
- Program Evaluations

Welcome

Welcome to RCL's *Reconciliation* sacrament preparation program. You will discover this is an exciting and comprehensive program that will help you guide children and young people as they prepare for a lifetime of being healed and forgiven in the sacrament of Reconciliation.

As Catholics we share in God's forgiveness and love each time we celebrate the sacrament of Reconciliation. It is within that liturgical experience that we come to know God's infinite mercy. Thus, RCL's sacrament preparation program uses liturgy as the starting point for catechesis.

This program director's manual contains a wealth of information. Take time to look at "About This Section" at the beginning of each section and discover the flexibility of this program. Within this resource you will find the materials and practical tools that can make your ministry easier. Whatever model or format your parish uses for sacrament preparation, RCL's *Reconciliation* program has been developed with you in mind.

As the program director, you are the one to whom people will look to for help and guidance during this time of sacrament preparation. You are the one who will energize and inspire parents, catechists, and your entire parish community. It is your privilege to join with all the faithful who will welcome these children and young people to a lifetime of being forgiven and healed in the sacrament of Reconciliation.

Models for Using the RCL Sacrament Preparation Program

Does your parish prepare children for the sacrament of Reconciliation with seven-, eight-, and nine-year-olds? Do you have older children you need to provide for in your sacrament preparation program?

Perhaps in your parish you have a sacrament preparation program that has a long history of success. The people in your parish are able to accommodate the schedule and requirements. Or perhaps you have been searching for a new and more effective approach to sacrament preparation.

Whatever your situation—searching or satisfied—RCL's *Reconciliation* program has been developed with you in mind. You will find that it is effective with any of the following models and options.

CHILD MODEL

- Child sessions are led by a teacher or a catechist.
- Child sessions are supplemented with parent meetings.

PARENT/CHILD MODEL

- Parents attend most or all sessions.
- Parents and children meet together in a parish or family cluster setting.
- Parents and children meet together for part of the session, and children meet with catechists for part of the session.

AT-HOME MODEL

- Parents and children participate in preparation sessions at home.
- Home sessions may be supplemented by gatherings in the parish setting of all the families with children preparing for sacraments.

Program Philosophy

RCL's *Reconciliation* sacrament preparation program is an extensive and comprehensive program designed to help guide children and young people as they prepare for a lifetime of being healed in the sacrament of Reconciliation.

The *Catechism of the Catholic Church* reminds us that our desire for God is written in our heart (CCC 27). This is true not only for adults but for children as well. Children are naturally spiritual and are drawn toward God.

As children approach the sacrament of Reconciliation, they are in the early stages of their spiritual journey. Thus, any adult—parent, catechist, or classroom teacher—is privileged to journey with the children during this time of preparation.

This preparation:

- is rooted in solid sacramental theology.

- includes the elements of ritual, prayer, Scripture, doctrine, and reflection.

- is centered in "the community, which lives, celebrates and bears witness to the faith" (*General Directory for Catechesis* 68).

The focus of this preparation is not only for "first" Reconciliation but more importantly for a lifetime of being healed and forgiven in the sacrament of Reconciliation. Such preparation is not only about cognitive learning but especially about a period of spiritual preparation.

The sacraments of Reconciliation and Anointing of the Sick are Sacraments of Healing. The Sacraments of Healing are Christ's way, through the Church, to do for us what we cannot do for ourselves: grant us complete and total forgiveness and restore us to hope.

By entering in the passion, death, and resurrection of Christ, the people of God become a sign in the world of conversion to God. All this the Church expresses in its life and celebrates in the liturgy (see *Rite of Penance* 4).

These few principles can guide us as we catechize children in preparation for the sacrament of Reconciliation.

- Sacraments are always a beginning. Children will grow in their understanding and experience of the sacraments as their faith deepens.

- Reconciliation is a sacrament that requires a basic understanding of right and wrong, mortal and venial sin, free will and the freedom to choose.

- The focus of this sacrament is on God's mercy and willingness to always forgive us. We need to be careful not to put all the focus on sin.

- It is through the power of the Holy Spirit that we are moved to sorrow for our sinfulness and are prompted to ask God's forgiveness.

Remember that in all we do we are preparing the children for a lifetime of being healed in the sacrament of Reconciliation.

Scope and Sequence

	CHAPTER 1 · We Belong to God	CHAPTER 2 · We Follow Jesus	CHAPTER 3 · We Listen to the Holy Spirit
Chapter Faith Theme	Baptism makes us sharers in divine life and marks us as belonging to Jesus the Good Shepherd.	The Great Commandment is a summary and the heart of all God's commandments.	The Holy Spirit helps us make good decisions and put them into action. In the confession of sins in Reconciliation we accept responsibility for our sins.
Ritual	*Blessing with water* • Celebrate the ritual actions of naming and blessing ourselves with water. • Reflect on important times we are called by name. • Discover and identify ways that praying the Sign of the Cross and blessing with water are part of our naming ourselves as Christians.	*Showing reverence for the word of God* • Celebrate the ritual action of gathering around the Bible, or Word of God, and processing. • Reflect on how gathering with people is part of daily living. • Discover and name ways that the Word of God is part of our living and celebrating our faith.	*Praying around a lighted candle* • Celebrate the ritual action of praying around a lighted candle. • Reflect on the ways families use lighted candles. • Discover and name ways that lighted candles help us celebrate and live our faith.
Scripture	*The Parable of the Lost Sheep—Luke 15:4–6* • Tell the story of the parable of the lost sheep. • Discover what it means to belong to God.	*The Great Commandment—Matthew 22:34–40* • Tell the story of Jesus teaching about the Great Commandment. • Discover what Jesus taught about showing reverence for God and for one another.	*The Parable of the Good Samaritan—Luke 10:29–37* • Tell the story of the parable of the Good Samaritan. • Discover the connection between the parable of the Good Samaritan and our call to live as followers of Jesus.
Doctrine/ Liturgy	*Sacrament of Baptism* • Jesus, the Good Shepherd, knows each of his sheep by name. He gave his life for us. Jesus' death and resurrection reveal how much God loves us. • At Baptism we are marked with the sign of the cross. This shows we belong to Christ and the Christian community. • Baptism joins us to Christ. God shares his life with us. We become adopted children of God and members of our church family. Original sin and all other sins are forgiven. We receive the gift of the Holy Spirit and the promise of eternal life.	*Overview of the Rites of Reconciliation* • We do what the Great Commandment tells us when we live the Ten Commandments. • God gives us the gifts of a conscience and a free will to live the Great Commandment. • Jesus gave us the sacraments to make us sharers in God's life. We can celebrate the sacrament of Penance, or Reconciliation, individually with the priest, or we can celebrate it together with other members of our church family and the priest. • In Reconciliation we are forgiven sins we commit after we have been baptized. We sin when we freely choose to do what we know is against God's commandments.	*The Confession of Sins* • We are lights in the world when we make good decisions and put them into action. Praying, listening to the word of God, learning what our church family teaches, and talking with a trustworthy adult help us make good decisions. • We sometimes do not make good decisions and we choose to sin. Confessing our sins in Reconciliation shows we want to do our best to live as Jesus taught. • In Reconciliation we confess, or tell, our sins to the priest. We must confess any mortal sin we may have committed. We may also confess venial sins.
What Difference Does This Make in My Life?	• Identify ways to share God's love with others. • Discover that sharing God's love with others makes a difference.	• Identify the people whom we know are living the Great Commandment. • Discover that living the Great Commandment makes a difference.	• Identify and choose ways to make good decisions and live as lights in the world. • Discover how bringing light to the world makes a difference.
Together as a Family	• Recall and talk about the child's baptism. • Identify and choose ways to live as signs of God's love as a family. • Review the meaning of the Sign of the Cross and include its praying in family prayers.	• Talk about ways family members can help one another live the Great Commandment. • Identify and choose ways to live as a forgiving family. • Briefly go through the ritual actions, prayers, and responses of the rite of Reconciliation.	• Share ideas on how our family can be a light in the world. • Pray as a family to the Holy Spirit. • Go through the ritual "Confession of Sins" in the rite of Reconciliation.

Chapter 4 • **We Are Sorry**	Chapter 5 • **We Are Forgiven**	Chapter 6 • **We Are Peacemakers**
We show our sorrow for our sins. The prayer of sorrow, or act of contrition, and penance express our decision and desire to heal the harm caused by our sins and to be reconciled with God and the Church.	In the sacrament of Reconciliation God forgives our sins through the ministry of bishops and priests.	The sacrament of Reconciliation makes us sharers in God's gift of peace and renews our calling to share that peace with others.
Praying the Our Father • Celebrate the ritual action of praying the Our Father. • Reflect on how praying is part of daily living. • Discover and name ways that showing we are sorry is part of living and celebrating our faith.	*Laying On of hands* • Celebrate the ritual action of laying on of hands. • Reflect on how making up, or reconciling, with others is part of daily living. • Discover and name ways reconciling with God and other people is part of living and celebrating our faith.	*Sharing a sign of peace* • Celebrate the ritual action of sharing a sign of peace. • Reflect on the ways that sharing peace is part of daily living. • Discover and name ways that sharing peace is part of living and celebrating our faith.
Zacchaeus—Luke 19:1–10 • Tell the story of the meeting between Jesus and the tax collector Zacchaeus. • Discover the connection between Zacchaeus showing people he was sorry and our living as a follower of Jesus.	*The Parable of the Forgiving Father—Luke 15:11–32* • Tell the parable of the forgiving father. • Discover the connection between this parable and God's love for us.	*The Gift of Peace—John 14:15–27 and 20:21* • Tell the story of the promise of Jesus to give his disciples the gift of peace. • Discover the connection between Jesus' promise and his presence with us.
Accepting a Penance and Praying the Act of Contrition • Being sorry is a sign of love. We need to express our sorrow for our sins. It shows our love for God and for other people. • The Holy Spirit helps us to be sorry for our sins. The Holy Spirit helps us to forgive others. • In the sacrament of Reconciliation accepting and doing our penance and praying an act of contrition shows we are sorry for our sins and helps us repair the harm we have caused by our sins.	*Absolution* • Reconciliation is one of the two Sacraments of Healing. • In this sacrament we share in God's mercy and forgiving love. Our sins are forgiven. The Holy Spirit reconciles us with God and with one another. • In the sacrament of Reconciliation Christ is present with the Church. Through the ministry of bishops and priests we are forgiven our sins. The bishop or priest absolves us from our sins "in the name of the Father, and of the Son, and of the Holy Spirit."	*Proclamation of Praise and Mercy/Dismissal* • Jesus taught that peacemakers are children of God. We live as peacemakers when we forgive others and ask others to forgive us. • At the end of the celebration of Reconciliation we are sent forth in peace. We are reconciled with God and with one another. We want everyone to know how wonderful God's love is.
• Identify and choose ways to show true sorrow. • Discover how showing true sorrow makes a difference.	• Identify times when we forgave others. • Discover how being forgiven and forgiving others makes a difference.	• Identify peacemakers we know and what they do. • Choose ways to live as a peacemaker and discover the difference living as a peacemaker makes.
• Talk about why expressing our sorrow is important for our family. • Go through the rituals "Receiving and Accepting a Penance" and "Praying an Act of Sorrow" in the rite of Reconciliation.	• Share ideas on ways our family can be a forgiving people. • Go through the ritual "Absolution" in the rite of Reconciliation.	• Share ideas on how family conflicts can be solved peacefully. • Go through the thanksgiving and dismissal rituals of the rite of Reconciliation.

Role of the Family, the Catechist, and the Assembly

Role of the Family

The Church views the role of parents in the religious formation of their children as both a privilege and an obligation. When Catholic parents present their children to the Church to be baptized, they are distinctly reminded that they have the responsibility "to bring [their children] up in the practice of the faith" (*Rite of Baptism of Children* 56).

This privilege and obligation extend to sacrament preparation. As parents present their children as candidates for first Reconciliation, they need to be incorporated into its overall vision and planning. It is important to remember that it has been within the family that children have first come to faith. And it is within that family setting that children will continue to practice their faith and witness the daily example of Catholic believers.

Pope John Paul in his 1994 Letter to Families reaffirmed the privileged responsibility of parents in the faith formation of their children. He wrote:

Parents are the first and most important educators of their own children, and they also possess a fundamental competence in this area: they are educators because they are parents (16).

Reaching out to families, the pope continued:
What I offer, then, is an invitation: an invitation addressed especially to you, dearly beloved husbands and wives, fathers and mothers, sons and daughters. It is an invitation to all the particular Churches to remain united in the teaching of the apostolic truth (23).

RCL's *Reconciliation* program recognizes the privileged place that parents have in the faith formation of their children. Reconciliation helps parents to meet their responsibilities "as the first and most important educators of their children" as they prepare their children not only for first Reconciliation but for a lifelong sharing in God's merciful love in the celebration of this sacrament.

How does the child's *Reconciliation* book include the family?

The child's *Reconciliation* book includes a "Together as a Family" section on the Scripture and doctrine pages in each chapter. In addition, an entire page is devoted to "Together as a Family" at the conclusion of each chapter. This page includes four parts:

- ● "Remember Together," which invites parents and children to share what they have learned as well as their own stories of faith.
- ● "Sharing Together," which provides suggestions for family activities.
- ● "Praying Together," which offers a simple prayer for the family to pray together.
- ● "Getting Ready Together," which gives practical suggestions of ways the family can prepare for first Reconciliation together.

Role of the Catechist

The catechist's role in sacrament preparation is one of spiritual guide, or companion on the journey. While cognitive learning is an important dimension of sacrament preparation, the real challenge and work of the catechist is to nurture each child's trust in the love and mercy of God, and to help them experience Jesus in their heart. The catechist will strive to achieve these goals by creating an environment that facilitates the children's experience of the love of God through Jesus Christ.

Role of the Assembly

The assembly plays an important role in preparing young people for sacraments. As members of the assembly we shape and form one another as we worship together. The *Rite of Christian Initiation of Adults* emphasizes that

the people of God, as represented by the local Church, should understand and show by their concern that . . . initiation . . . is the responsibility of all the baptized (9).

The *Reconciliation Program Director's Manual* provides tools and resources to enhance the role of the assembly in leading others to complete their initiation into the Church.

Dear Parents,

It probably seems like only yesterday that you presented your child for Baptism. At that time, those gathered—speaking for all the faithful—spoke their willingness to journey with you as you brought your child up in faith. Today, as you journey with your child to first Reconciliation, the community of faith is at your side.

As parents you have a unique role in the religious formation of your child. The Church views your role as both a privilege and a responsibility. This privilege and responsibility both extend to sacrament preparation. It is within your family that your child has first come to faith. It is within your family that your child will continue to live out faith and witness the daily example of Catholic believers.

Your child's *Reconciliation* book provides many opportunities for you to share in this time of sacrament preparation. The Scripture and doctrine pages in each chapter include a "Together as a Family" section, which offers suggestions for home use. In addition, an entire page is devoted to "Together as a Family" at the end of each chapter. This page includes four parts:

- "Remember Together," which invites you to discuss what was learned and to share your own stories of faith with your child.

- "Sharing Together," which provides suggestions for family activities.

- "Praying Together," which offers a simple prayer for your family to pray together at mealtimes or other family times of prayer.

- "Getting Ready Together," which gives some practical suggestions on ways you can prepare for first Reconciliation together.

As you share in this blessed time of sacrament preparation, enjoy the time you and your child spend together. Keep your child in your prayers as you, together with the entire Christian community, welcome your child to a lifetime of being forgiven and healed in the sacrament of Reconciliation.

Guidelines for Planning the Celebration of the Sacraments

All planning for the celebration of the sacraments would be in collaboration with the liturgist and the presider in your community. Here are some suggested guidelines to assist you in the planning process.

When to Celebrate

The season of Lent is most appropriate for celebrating the sacrament of Reconciliation. A communal celebration of the sacrament would be appropriate.

Final Preparation for Candidates

Candidates should be well-prepared members of the assembly. This means that they should be familiar with the responses and acclamations. If there will be a rehearsal, keep it simple and practice only what is absolutely necessary.

Preparation for Ministers

Liturgical roles (readers, greeters, and so on) would be best kept with members of the assembly who have been trained and commissioned, and who claim this as their ministry.

Readings and Gospel

The readings and Gospel should be from the suggested readings found in the ritual text of the *Rite of Penance*.

Environment

The environment for the liturgy should reflect the liturgical season. If you are using a reconciliation room, see that it is uncluttered and well arranged. It is best to keep things simple and focused. If you are setting up stations around the church, make sure you offer distance from the assembly to insure privacy.

Engaging the Assembly

All through this sacrament preparation program, the assembly has had the opportunity to be connected to those preparing for the sacrament. The celebration should acknowledge the work of the assembly in the preparation.

Music

RCL's *Reconciliation* music CD, which accompanies this sacrament program, has many songs, hymns, and acclamations that would be appropriate for the liturgy. The music should be familiar to those celebrating the sacrament.

Rite for Reconciliation of Several Penitents with Individual Confession and Absolution

Use this worksheet for planning the liturgy, making music selections,
scheduling ministers, planning choreography, and so on. It is also helpful
to refer to the *Rite of Penance* for suggestions.

Highlight symbols—candle, cross, Bible, laying on of hands

Outline of the Ritual

Introductory Rites

    Song _____
    See *Rite of Penance* 48

    Greeting _____
    See *Rite of Penance* 49

    Opening Prayer _____
    See *Rite of Penance* 50

Celebration of the Word of God

    Readings _____
    See *Rite of Penance* 53

    Homily _____
    See *Rite of Penance* 52

Examination of Conscience _____
See *Rite of Penance* 53
or you may use the child's book, page 64.

Rite for Reconciliation

    General Confession of Sins _____
    See *Rite of Penance* 54

    Litany or Song and Lord's Prayer _____
    See *Rite of Penance* 54

    Individual Confession and Absolution _____
    See *Rite of Penance* 55

    Proclamation of Praise for God's Mercy _____
    See *Rite of Penance* 56

    Concluding Prayer of Thanksgiving _____
    See *Rite of Penance* 57

Concluding Rite _____
See *Rite of Penance* 58–59

Professional Articles

These articles can be used to enrich your own background, catechist training, parent meetings, adult education, parish resources, parish/school staff development, pastoral council formation, liturgy committee updating, and for reprint in the parish bulletin or parish newsletter.

Readiness for the Sacraments

A child, whether that child is seven years old, eight years old, nine years old, or older, is only capable of age-appropriate readiness for participation in the celebration of the sacrament of Penance. A seven-year-old can only understand God's mercy and forgiveness as a seven-year-old. Furthermore, a child's ability to comprehend such concepts as conscience, temptation, intention, and sin—both mortal sin and venial sin—is also limited by age and moral development. As the child grows in knowledge and faith, his or her understanding and appreciation of the sacrament of Reconciliation will naturally deepen.

What about the Moral Development of Children?

Moral development occurs gradually over many years, and it is difficult to predict with precision just when particular moral stages will occur. The following generalizations provide some insight into the moral development of children and will help you appreciate that development:

- Prior to the age of eight or nine, children may have difficulty distinguishing between mistakes they have made, what has occurred accidentally, and what they have willfully done.

- Prior to the age of eight or nine, children have two standards for determining when sin is serious, or mortal. One standard is the intensity of the adult reaction to the event. The other is the quantity or volume involved, for example, the number of items versus the value of the items stolen.

- The intention to do wrong—that is essential to sinful action—is often beyond a child's understanding. Children will eventually realize that they must intend to act sinfully in order for their act to be a sin.

- Because of the very nature of children, they often do not think before they act. When a child says, "I didn't mean to do it," they are probably telling the truth. They simply did not stop to think. Adults need to remind children often to stop and think before they act.

- Adults can help children reflect on their actions by calmly asking the child: Why did you do that? What did you think would happen? Did you realize what you were doing was wrong or sinful? Did you intend to act sinfully? What can you do to keep from doing this again?

What are Reasonable Expectations for a Child's Readiness?

Several reasonable expectations that point to a child's readiness are:

- It is reasonable to expect that the child has been participating in Sunday Mass on a regular basis.

- It is reasonable to expect that the child has been participating in ongoing catechesis and will continue to do so.

- It is reasonable to expect that prayer is a part of the child's life, and is experienced within the family as well as within the Church.

- It is reasonable to expect that the child can recognize the difference between right and wrong.

- It is important that the child know the difference between accidents or mistakes and freely choosing a sinful behavior.

- It is important that the child understand what constitutes mortal and venial sin.

- It is reasonable to expect that the child has the capacity for sincere sorrow and can make an honest effort to do better.

- It is important that the child understand that God will always forgive us—all we need to do is ask.

Dioceses and parishes may vary in their readiness requirements for children approaching the sacrament of Penance for the first time. Whatever the standard of readiness your diocese and parish establish, be certain that the child is never led to believe that he or she has to earn the privilege of sharing in God's mercy and forgiveness in the sacrament of Reconciliation.

Learning the History
THE ESSENTIAL PARTS OF THE SACRAMENT

Catholics know that our rituals for the sacraments have undergone a process of evolution and development over the centuries.

No one imagines that the pope celebrates Mass today in exactly the same way as Saint Peter presided over the eucharistic gatherings of early Christians in Rome. How we baptize an adult candidate today is quite different from the scenes described in the Acts of the Apostles, where sudden conversions and riverside baptisms appear to be considered quite normal. Despite the changing shape of the Church's sacramental rituals across the centuries, we also recognize a continuity in the essentials of each of the sacraments.

Periods of Development of the Sacrament of Penance

No sacrament has had more change in its external ritual and pastoral practice over the centuries than the sacrament of Penance. Historians of the sacrament identify broad periods during which the practice of reconciling sinners to the Church underwent significant evolution and change. These periods are:

Early Christianity—We have little by way of historical evidence about the ways that the Church reconciled sinners after Baptism in the first centuries. What we know for certain is that the gospel message of Christ's forgiveness was strongly felt and practiced, that bishops took a strong leadership role in calling the faithful to conversion and reconciling them when they strayed, and that prayer for forgiveness in the midst of the community was central to the Church's healing ministry.

Canonical Penance—During the fourth through sixth centuries a system of canonical penance developed, which included a formal structure called the Order of Penitents. Enrollment in this process was public and involved doing public (and sometimes very lengthy) acts of reparation for serious sins. Reconciliation was at the hands of the bishop who eventually (sometimes not until the penitent was on his or her deathbed) readmitted the sinner to the sacraments of the Church. The length and severity of this form of penance contributed to the development of "deathbed penance," a practice of delaying one's request for sacramental reconciliation until one was near death.

Monastic (Tariff) Penance—During the sixth through ninth centuries another, more gentle way of reconciling sinners developed primarily in monastic communities. Related to spiritual direction, with its emphasis on healing weakness and developing the life of virtue, this system was more private and individualistic than its predecessor, focusing very much on specific sinful acts being matched by specific acts of penance. The legalistic tracking of these tariffs led to abuses, and an absence of formal ritual also weakened this practice and prepared the way for what we know today as our modern practice.

Modern Penance—Since the dawn of the second millennium, the Church's practice of the sacrament of Penance has developed into what we today popularly call confession. Each prior period of history contributed to the evolution of this sacrament. By the time of the Council of Trent in the sixteenth century, the Church was in a position to offer a clear teaching on what constitutes the essential parts, or elements, of the sacrament, regardless of how the sacrament may be practiced during changing historical circumstances.

Reflection on these essential parts of the sacrament of Penance allows us to recognize that these essential elements have indeed always been at work in the history of the Church. Our reflection also allows us to deepen our appreciation for (and practice of) each dimension of the sacrament as we seek a contemporary renewal of penance and reconciliation in the Church of the third millennium.

Essential Elements of the Sacrament of Penance

There are four essential elements of the sacrament of Penance that have been consistently part of the celebration of this sacrament.

Contrition—True sorrow for sin, or contrition, is at the heart of the sacrament. Without genuine sorrow and a desire to change one's life, a person who seeks reconciliation is actually closed to God's offer of forgiveness. Jesus' preaching of conversion (see Mark 1:15) is at the core of the gospel message—the offer of God's forgiving love to one and all alike. In every age and under every circumstance, contrition is the bedrock foundation for the Church's celebration of Penance.

Confession—The public disclosure of one's sinfulness constitutes the second essential element in the Church's practice of Penance. Whether this confession be through an enrollment in a public

> **"** Jesus' preaching of conversion is at the core of the gospel message— the offer of God's forgiving love to one and all alike. **"**

Order of Penitents or in the privileged confidence shared with a monastic guide, whether it be in a confessional box that proliferated after the Council of Trent or in the relaxed atmosphere of many contemporary celebrations of communal penance, the Church has always insisted that one admit to being a sinner if there is to be true forgiveness and reconciliation.

Acts of Penance (Satisfaction)—Doing penance for one's sins is a necessary expression of sorrow. The severity of public penance in the early centuries has been replaced today by a more symbolic acceptance of the penance that the priest gives in the sacrament. In former times we ran the risk of excessive severity; today we risk superficiality and trivializing penance. What is called for in every age is the change of one's life that is the ultimate purpose of the sacrament. Whether penance is done before the ritual is celebrated (as in the Canonical Penance) or after (as is done today), the Church insists that one make external (by our human acts) the interior, invisible change of heart worked by God's grace in the sacrament.

Absolution—The final essential element identified by the Council of Trent is the priest's prayer of absolution. Speaking in the name of Christ ("I absolve . . .") and on behalf of the Church, the priest pronounces God's forgiveness for our sins and formally reconciles the sinner to the Church from which he or she has strayed. The ritual of the sacrament reaches its climactic moment as the sacred words of absolution are pronounced over one who has true sorrow, has confessed sinfulness, and has willingly accepted the satisfaction offered by the priest.

For Reflection

How does the history of the sacrament of Penance affect your understanding of the sacrament?

What is the connection between Baptism and Penance?

Given the history of the sacrament, what do you see as the future for the sacrament of Penance?

The Paths of Forgiveness
THE MANY WAYS GOD'S FORGIVENESS TOUCHES OUR LIVES

Those who practice the Jesus Prayer of the Eastern Church pray incessantly, "Lord Jesus, have mercy on me a sinner." This prayer wells up from a heart completely convinced of one's utter and fundamental dependence on the mercy of God for the whole of our existence.

Shortly before his death, Thomas Merton summarized Christian consciousness as the awareness of being a forgiven sinner. We have sinned, and we cannot act or behave as if we have not. There is no room for presumption.

At the same time, we are forgiven by God's mercy. So there is no room for endless, numbing, nonproductive guilt and self-recrimination. God gives real forgiveness and new life.

Forgiveness is central in the Christian experience. Yet Christians have not always clearly understood the paths of forgiveness, the ways that God's forgiveness takes hold of their lives. This essay attempts to look at and organize the ways that God's forgiveness comes to us: where it begins, how it unfolds, and what personal response it evokes from us.

The one way of forgiveness: The cross of Jesus Christ

Only God can forgive sins (see Mark 2:7). Indeed, God has forgiven our sins through the sacrificial death of Jesus on the cross. Jesus told his disciples, "This is my blood of the covenant, which is poured out for many" (Mark 14:24).

Saint Paul described this great forgiveness and reconciliation to his beloved Church in Corinth. Paul wrote:

So if anyone is in Christ, there is a new creation: everything old has passed away; see, everything has become new! All this is from God, who reconciled us to himself through Christ, and given us the ministry of reconciliation; that is, in Christ God was reconciling the world to himself, not counting their trespasses against them, and entrusting the message of reconciliation to us. . . . For our sake he made him to be sin who knew no sin, so that in him we might become the righteousness of God.

2 Corinthians 5:17–19, 21

Access to the grace of forgiveness and reconciliation

On the day of Pentecost, Peter, made bold by the outpouring of the Holy Spirit, preached the basic Christian message, concluding with these words:

"God has made him both Lord and Messiah, this Jesus whom you crucified."

Acts of the Apostles 2:36

Saint Luke then describes the listeners' reaction as being "cut to the heart" (2:37), and their immediate question was about access to this grace of forgiveness.

[They] said to Peter and to the other apostles, "Brothers, what should we do?"

Acts of the Apostles 2:37

Peter's response is very telling, because it lays out the fundamental path, or access, to God's forgiveness in Jesus Christ. He says:

"Repent, and be baptized every one of you in the name of Jesus Christ so that your sins may be forgiven; and you will receive the gift of the Holy Spirit."

Acts of the Apostles 2:38

Baptism, then, is the fundamental sacrament of forgiveness—that point of transforming encounter with the merciful Lord who both forgives our sins and gives us new life, the gift of the Holy Spirit.

The sacrament of Penance presupposes Baptism and is based on Baptism. The sacrament of Penance is for those who after Baptism have sinned and lost the grace of new life in the Holy Spirit (sanctifying grace) and have wounded ecclesial communion (the Body of Christ) to whom they were joined in baptism. Canon 960 expresses this same thought:

Individual and integral confession and absolution are the sole ordinary means by which the faithful, conscious of grave sin, are reconciled with God and the Church.

In answer, then, to the question of access to God's forgiveness, we can say that Baptism is the first and fundamental way that God forgives us. In the case of serious sin after Baptism, the sacrament of Reconciliation is the ordinary means for receiving God's forgiveness.

The Other Sacraments and Forgiveness

Other sacraments besides Penance extend the forgiving grace of Baptism or even, in necessity, renew it. For example, the ritual for the Anointing of the Sick, citing the Council of Trent, identifies this effect of that sacrament:

If necessary, the sacrament also provides the sick person with the forgiveness of sins and the completion of Christian penance. *Rite of Anointing of the Sick* 6

The *Catechism of the Catholic Church* (CCC) teaches that the Eucharist forgives sin by strengthening in us the virtue of charity, thus wiping away venial sins (see CCC 1394). Concerning serious sin, the *Catechism* states that while serious sin is not forgiven by our sharing in Eucharist, the Eucharist does strengthen us and preserves us from future mortal sins. The ordinary path for the forgiveness of serious, or mortal, sin is the sacrament of Reconciliation (see CCC 1395).

The Human Response to God's Forgiveness and the Virtue of Penance

The sacramental paths of forgiveness highlight the primacy of God's action in us—the absolute priority of the grace, or gift, of God's forgiveness made accessible and tangible for us in an objective way through the sacraments. There is, in addition to this objective way, a subjective side—a way that we personalize and take into ourselves this grace of forgiveness. This is the virtue of penance, which the

German theologian Karl Rahner describes in this way:

Penance as a virtue denotes the morally and religiously appropriate human attitude, bestowed by the grace of Christ, in regard to one's own sin and to sin generally.
The Concise Sacramentum Mundi 1187

In other words, we cultivate the habitual awareness of who we are as sinners and of who God is as the one who forgives us.

Sometimes this subjective, personal sense of penance and repentance leads us to the celebration of the sacrament of Reconciliation. Sometimes the celebration of this sacrament leads us to this more personal awareness. In either case, the virtue of penance leads us to living out a continuous conversion of heart, a constant sense of life held in the forgiving mercy of God.

Practices of the Virtue of Penance

We find conversion and forgiveness—as prelude and as consequence of our sacramental life—in various penitential practices. The ancient and traditional triad of penitential practices includes fasting, prayer, and almsgiving, or care of the poor.

The *Catechism* elaborates on the role of the practice of the virtue of penance in our life of conversion. It teaches that conversion is accomplished gradually in daily life through living the corporal and spiritual works of mercy and the Beatitudes, including such works as reaching out to the poor, the

practical commitment to justice, the loving correction of our brothers and sisters, the acknowledgment and admission of our faults and need for conversion, the acceptance of suffering and the endurance of persecution for the sake of righteousness, and the taking up of one's cross each day (see CCC 1435).

Conclusion

Jesus proclaimed the greatness of God's merciful love. Jesus Christ is the way to this divine mercy and forgiveness. The Letter to the Ephesians reminds us:

But God, who is rich in mercy, out of the great love with which he loved us even when we were dead through our trespasses, made us alive together with Christ. Ephesians 2:4

God's mercy is indeed rich, and the paths of forgiveness are many—from the grace of Baptism and the sacrament of Reconciliation to the personal practices and pleas of a contrite heart.

For Reflection

Which pathway to forgiveness are you most familiar with? Which pathway is new to you?

How do the various pathways to forgiveness affect your understanding of God's forgiveness?

Which pathway to forgiveness is emphasized in your parish community? Which pathway needs greater exposure?

An "Uninterrupted Task"
CONTINUING CONVERSION AND CONSCIENCE FORMATION

Saint Ambrose, the fourth-century bishop of Milan, wrote eloquently of our need for conversion and repentance.

In the Church, Ambrose wrote, "there are water and tears: the water of Baptism and the tears of repentance" (Letter 41). These "tears of repentance" are indicative of what the *Catechism of the Catholic Church* (CCC 1428) calls a Christian's *second conversion.*

A Life of Continuing Conversion to Christ

Christ continuously calls the baptized to conversion. The conversion of the baptized to Christ is a lifelong and uninterrupted task of the whole Church who, "clasping sinners to her bosom, [is] at once holy and always in need of purification, [and] follows constantly the path of penance and renewal" (DOGMATIC CONSTITUTION ON THE CHURCH [LUMEN GENTIUM] 8.3 IN CCC 1428).

We have ample evidence that the Church, although embracing within itself the very holiness of Christ, nonetheless is filled with sinners. Both the Church as an institution and we as individuals need constantly to hear and respond to Christ's call to conversion.

In the Introduction to the *Rite of Penance,* there is an indication of some of the many ways that Christians seek this continual process of repentance:

They share in the sufferings of Christ (see 1 Peter 4:13) by enduring their own difficulties, carry out works of mercy and charity (see 1 Peter 4:8), and adopt ever more fully the outlook of the Gospel message. . . . [The Church celebrates this repentance] in penitential services, in the proclamation of the word of God, in prayer, and in the penitential parts of the eucharistic celebration. *RITE OF PENANCE 4*

In its most solemn form, this *second conversion* is ritualized in the sacrament of Penance. Even when it is not a question of serious sin that bars one from the sacraments and requires sacramental absolution, tradition has developed the practice of devotional confession. Indicating the benefit of this kind of celebration, the *Rite of Penance* insists:

This is not a mere ritual repetition or psychological exercise, but a serious striving to perfect the grace of baptism so that, as we bear in our body the death of Jesus Christ, his life may be seen in us ever more clearly (see 2 Corinthians 4:10). . . . [Thus are we] more closely conformed to Christ and . . . follow the voice of the Spirit more attentively.

In order that this sacrament of healing may truly achieve its purpose among the faithful, it must take root in their entire life and move them to more fervent service of God and neighbor. *RITE OF PENANCE 7*

The Formation of Conscience and the Call to Conversion

In order to help the sacrament of Penance "take root in their entire life," children need to be formed not only in the mechanics of how to celebrate the sacrament but also in the spirit of repentance that responds to Jesus' gospel call for conversion. The formation of conscience is an extremely important element in this task, not only as a young person prepares for first Penance, but throughout the childhood years of growth and development.

The demands of continuing conversion require that even after the celebration of Penance for the first time, children receive ongoing guidance and formation of conscience. See the articles in RCL's *Reconciliation Catechist Guide* and in this program director's manual that discuss the moral development of the child as one aspect of readiness for the sacrament.

> " Spiritual formation and the development of a good conscience go hand in hand as one learns to love God and neighbor throughout the formative years of childhood. "

There is substantial literature in the field of developmental psychology that details the stages of cognitive development through which a child passes on the way to adulthood. It is very important to understand these stages, lest we think a child's understanding is capable of more (or less) than is developmentally appropriate at any given age.

The intellectual categories by which a child understands sin, forgiveness, grace, even God, change and develop as a child grows. Parents and educators need to keep pace with that evolving consciousness and help children internalize the moral teachings of the Church at successively more complex and developed levels of understanding.

The Spiritual Life and the Spiritual Formation of a Child

Even deeper than the development of cognitive categories in which a child formulates matters of conscience, we must nurture the child's growing relationship with God, a relationship that we refer to comprehensively with the term "spiritual life." The insights of Robert Coles in his books *The Spiritual Life of Children* and *The Moral Intelligence of Children* are sufficient to astound us at the depth and breadth of a child's relationship with God, even when that relationship is expressed in intellectual categories that are relatively unsophisticated.

Parents and educators need to make certain that a child is exposed to a rich fabric of faith both at home and in parish settings, a faith openly shared, celebrated, and acted upon in daily life. Blessed are the children whose parents appropriately invite them into their own moral struggles, into perspectives on daily life that are value-laden and seen through the perspective of Catholic faith.

A child's spiritual life is enriched and conscience is formed in moments of family prayer, when parents reconcile with one another after tempers flare, and when unconditional love is experienced firsthand, even in the face of childhood transgressions.

Values are internalized and consciences allowed to mature when parental strictures are gradually eased in a way proportionate to developing maturity, when trust in a child is reinforced even in the face of mistakes committed. Saying to a child, "What did you learn from your mistake?" is much more productive of a mature conscience than, "You're grounded!"

Telling a child who has sinned, "I still love you, and so does God!" enriches the child's spiritual life far more than, "Shame on you! Imagine how you've hurt God by your bad behavior!"

The second conversion which the *Catechism* refers to as an uninterrupted task must be supported in many ways as a child grows and develops. Spiritual formation and the development of a good conscience go hand in hand as one learns to love God and neighbor throughout the formative years of childhood. Parents and educators—indeed, the entire Christian community—conspire, by the example of their own lives as well as by their formal efforts, to lead the child into the mystery of God's love.

For Reflection

How does the sacrament of Penance encourage ongoing conversion?

What do I do to continue to form my own conscience?

In what ways can the church community assist with continuing conversion and conscience formation?

Sin and Grace

You can spot a Catholic who has "retired" for some time from going to Mass, when they excuse themselves, saying, "Oh, I don't go to Mass because of all the fire and brimstone preaching." Anyone who has gone to Mass in the last thirty years has not heard much fire and brimstone. In fact, they have not heard much at all about sin and guilt and punishment.

What Happened to Sin and Guilt?

Perhaps it is the expectations of the therapeutic society in which we live that discourages us from even thinking or talking about sin and failure and guilt. We may be afraid of damaging people's self-esteem, including our own. Or maybe it has to do with the pendular swings that have always been in play, as Pope John Paul II alluded in a recent letter to priests about the sacrament of Reconciliation. The pope wrote:

> It is a ministry always beset by two opposite extremes: severity and laxity. . . . We must always be careful to maintain a proper balance in order to avoid falling into one or the other of these extremes. Severity crushes people and drives them away. Laxity is misleading and deceptive (see JOHN PAUL II, *LETTER TO PRIESTS FOR HOLY THURSDAY*, 2002.)

The sacrament of forgiveness makes no sense if there is nothing to forgive, so we need an authentic understanding of sin. On the other hand, the sacrament of mercy makes no sense if we seem stuck in sin, guilt, and fear with no way out. Thus we need an authentic sense of the forgiving, healing grace that is available to us in the sacrament. Where do we begin?

At the Dawn of Human History

The Church holds that at the dawn of human history our first parents made a disobedient choice. They made a deliberate act of distancing and alienating themselves from God, which we call original sin. They did so, responding to a voice opposed to God who would put them into opposition to God (see Genesis 3:1–5).

> **"**Our first parents made . . . a deliberate act of distancing and alienating themselves from God, which we call original sin. They did so, responding to a voice opposed to God who would put them into opposition to God.**"**

Scripture and the Church's Tradition see in this being a fallen angel, called "Satan" or the "devil." The real devil does not match our Hollywood-formed imaginations. The reality is far less showy but far more sinister and destructive. The devil is called in Greek *diabolos*, the one who engages in *dia-ballein*, splitting and separating, causing divisions and seeking to put distance between us and God and one another.

In the Bible the devil is also called "the father of lies," the great deceiver. These are the principal works of the devil— splitting and deceiving, dividing and misrepresenting. And they are the sources of temptations that lead us into sin.

Effects of Original Sin in our own Lives Today

We carry the effects of original sin within ourselves. The Second Vatican Council taught that the human person is divided within himself or herself. This division gives rise to the many painful and serious divisions in society and in today's world (see PASTORAL CONSTITUTION ON THE CHURCH IN THE MODERN WORLD [*GAUDIUM ET SPES*] 10).

Saint Paul described this experience of the divided self, unable to accept and live out the truth:

> I do not do the good I want, but the evil I do not want is what I do. Now if I do what I do not want, it is no longer I that do it, but sin that dwells in me.
> So I find it to be a law that when I want to do what is good, evil lies close at hand. For

I delight in the law of God in my inmost self, but I see in my members another law at war with the law of my mind, making me captive to the law of sin that dwells in my members. ROMANS 7:19–23

Paul's self-reflections and the Church's teaching about the inner division of the human person are very important. They tell us that even before we commit sins, we are sinners—a people of divided heart who do not clearly grasp the truth.

Thus, we are susceptible to the devil's temptations. To name ourselves as sinners expresses a significant dimension of our identity, our identity that needs to be healed and transformed. The power of the sacrament, then, not only forgives what we have done but heals us in our very woundedness.

Sin—Taking What is not God and Making It God

We not only are sinners but also do commit sin—acts or omissions that can essentially alienate us from God and also from one another. In a general way, Saint Augustine described sin as *aversio a Deo et conversio ad creaturam*, "a turning away from God and a turning to a creature."

Augustine's wise intuition was that all sin was fundamentally idolatry: we take what is not God and make it our god. This matches the closing and powerful words of the First Letter of John:

[W]e are in him who is true, in his Son Jesus Christ. He is the true God and eternal life.

Little children, keep yourselves from idols. 1 JOHN 5:20B–21

The idols that we construct or the creatures to which we so ardently attach ourselves can be our very selves or our pleasure or our convenience or our possessions or our security or our image.

In short, the Ten Commandments, the words of the prophets, and the warnings of Jesus make us look at what we have turned to, attached ourselves to, and allowed our lives to be led by. If this is not God, then we commit sin, both by our acts and by our omissions.

This talk of sin is very personal, but no sin remains private and individual. We affect each other inevitably. Personal sin invades the social order of things and leads to sinful injustice and merciless oppression.

God's Grace—the More Powerful and Ultimately Triumphant Reality

It is necessary to identify sin in its roots, in its essence, and in its manifestations. At the same time, if we are to be true to our biblical traditions and the very best of our spiritual traditions, we will never speak of sin alone.

For the people of faith, sin is always taken up into the larger, more powerful, and ultimately triumphant reality of God's merciful and forgiving grace. This is the pattern of Saint Paul's preaching and teaching, and we ought to follow it.

[All] have sinned and fall short of the glory of God; they are now justified by his grace as a gift, through the redemption that is in Christ Jesus. ROMANS 3:23–24

And later in the same letter, Paul writes:

Wretched man that I am! Who will rescue me from this body of death? Thanks be to God through Jesus Christ our Lord! ROMANS 7:24–25A

We must honestly face the realities of sin and grace if we are to make sense of our lives in faith. We then begin to understand the healing, forgiving, and transforming purpose of the sacrament of Reconciliation.

The matter is not so complicated, and it is certainly not remote. Indeed, it is as close to us as our daily prayer that breathes the very spirit of the sacrament: forgive us our trespasses, lead us not into temptation, but deliver us from evil.

For Reflection

What does it mean to have a healthy sense of sin?

What does it mean to be a "graced" sinner?

What does it mean that we are a community of "wounded" healers?

The Sacrament of Reconciliation
THE CHURCH'S PRACTICE AND UNDERSTANDING OF THE SACRAMENT

Among the paradoxes of American life today, the disparity between the secular confession of sin and the religious confession of sin is among the most puzzling—and especially perplexing—for people committed to the Church's mission and ministry of reconciliation.

The Current Atmosphere

On a daily basis people confess the lurid (and often sinful) details of their lives on TV talk shows. Individuals and insurance companies pay huge sums for therapy and counseling that often involve the disclosure of moral failures and the deep divisions and brokenness of the human heart.

At the same time, fewer and fewer Catholics seem to avail themselves of the sacrament of Reconciliation. Since the early 1980s Pope John Paul II has spoken of "a crisis of the sacrament," a situation the pope addressed in April 2002 in *On Certain Aspects of the Celebration of the Sacrament of Penance* [Misericordia Dei].

In *Novo millennio ineunte* the Holy Father had requested that priests, deacons, religious education teachers and directors, and other lay ecclesial ministers strengthen their pastoral efforts to renew participation in this sacrament. He wrote:

I am . . . asking for renewed pastoral courage in ensuring that the day-to-day teaching of Christian communities persuasively and effectively presents the practice of the Sacrament of Reconciliation."

NOVO MILLENNIO INEUNTE, 37

The Practice of the Sacrament

Although the practice, or form, of the sacrament has varied over history (see "Learning the History: The Essential Parts of the Sacrament" in this manual), there are four constant elements, or acts of the penitent and the confessor, that have always, in one way or another, marked the Church's practice of this sacrament. These elements are:

- The penitent, moved by God's grace, feels sorrow or contrition for sins committed and desires to change. That contrition is expressed in the sacramental encounter.

- The penitent confesses sins to the priest, that is, with specificity the penitent names and numbers those serious, or mortal, sins that have broken one's relationship with God; less serious sins, or venial sins, may also be confessed profitably.

- The penitent enacts satisfaction for the sins committed. For example, if the penitent has stolen something, it is to be returned. Even beyond such forms of physical restitution, there is also a spiritual satisfaction that needs to be accomplished, a penance given by the confessor that addresses the consequences of sin.

- The confessor receives the confession of sins. He serves as a judge who accepts the sincere confession of sins made by the penitent and then pronounces, in the name of Christ and by the power of the Holy Spirit, a judgment of mercy, the forgiveness of sins in the prayer of absolution. The confessor also serves as a physician who in giving a penance and advice seeks the healing of the penitent.

The *Rite of Penance* currently provides for three forms for the celebration of the sacrament of Reconciliation:

- The rite for reconciliation of individual penitents (individual confession and absolution)

- The rite for reconciliation of several penitents with individual confession and absolution

- The rite for reconciliation of several penitents with general confession and absolution

> **"** Pope John Paul II has spoken of 'a crisis of the sacrament.' **"**

Although the *Rite of Penance* lists the last rite, which has come to be known as Form Three, along with the other two, the Church views this rite as "an extraordinary means to be used in wholly exceptional situations" *(Misericordia Dei)*. In his teaching about "Form Three" in *Misericordia Dei,* the Holy Father cites the *Code of Canon Law* of the Church on this matter:

> Individual and integral confession and absolution are the sole ordinary means by which the faithful, conscious of grave sin, are reconciled with God and the Church; only physical or moral impossibility excuses from such confession, in which case reconciliation can be obtained in other ways. CANON 960

When general confession and absolution are given in an emergency or mission land situation, certain conditions are to be observed. The Holy Father, once again referring the *Code of Canon Law,* states:

> For the faithful to avail themselves validly of sacramental absolution given to many at one time, it is required that they not only be suitably disposed but also at the time intend to confess individually the serious sins which at present cannot be so confessed. CODE 962

Another significant and long-standing direction from Canon Law concerning the sacrament of Reconciliation is the obligation "to confess serious sins at least once a year" (Code 989). This, along with the "Easter duty," the obligation to receive the Eucharist at least once during the Lenten-Easter season, identifies a baseline minimum of sacramental practice for Catholics.

Understanding the Practice of the Church

A question often raised by non-Catholics and, increasingly, by Catholics themselves is, Why confess your sins to a priest? That seemingly simple question brings us into the heart of our faith convictions about sacramental life.

Christ has entrusted his gifts of mercy and forgiveness to the Church. This is the way the Church has understood the words of the Risen Christ: "[H]e breathed on them and said to them, 'Receive the Holy Spirit. If you forgive the sins of any, they are forgiven them; and if you retain the sins of any, they are retained' " (John 20:22–23).

The mediation of God's forgiveness through the Church takes specific shape in the sacramental encounter of priest and penitent. In this sacrament, properly celebrated and with all the proper dispositions, we are assured of receiving God's forgiveness. This is a very important faith conviction.

The sacrament is not just about subjective feelings of remorse and a personal conviction of forgiveness, although these certainly may be a part of it. The sacrament is about an objective, real, and effective word of forgiveness spoken in the name of Jesus, namely, "I absolve you from your sins," by the power of the Holy Spirit. The sacrament is not just a declaration of forgiveness, a proclamation of God's word, but the action of God working through the Church and the priest to forgive and heal a penitent sinner.

In this way the sacrament offers us some objective assurance that we are touched by God's merciful forgiveness. This is the fundamental response to why we confess to a priest.

The sacrament seems to center on sin—its confession and its forgiveness. In fact, in the style of Saint Paul (see Romans 5:15–21), sin in the sacramental context is really an occasion to meet the mercy of God, the true center of the sacrament.

Pope John Paul II calls insistently "for a rediscovery of Christ as *mysterium pietatis,* the one in whom God shows us his compassionate heart and reconciles us fully with himself. It is this face of Christ that must be rediscovered through the Sacrament of Penance" (NOVO MILLENNIO INEUNTE 37).

For Reflection

What element in the sacrament of Reconciliation is most meaningful to you? Why?

How do you explain to non-Catholics why Catholics confess to a priest?

For you, is mercy or sin the focus of the sacrament? Why?

The Church as a Reconciled and Reconciling Community

Whether the place for confession is a confessional box or a nicely appointed reconciliation room, the tone is always hushed and communication is often in whispers. For good reasons—shame and embarrassment, for example—we would rather not broadcast our sins. Yet the whole process of reconciliation, and perhaps its greatest challenge, leads us to recognize that it is no mere personal or private affair.

Reconciliation: A Communal Event

We bring our sins to the Church, the community to which we belong and the community to which the Lord Jesus entrusted a reconciling mission and ministry. We know that even the most private and hidden sins can have enormous repercussions in the life of the Church, as instances of clergy misconduct sadly attest. We know, as the *Catechism of the Catholic Church* reminds us, that our reconciliation with the Church is inseparable from our reconciliation with God (CCC 1445).

There is a way that reconciliation both as a sacrament and as a more general mission and ministry is profoundly social and ecclesial. It belongs to the very nature and life of the Church to be both a reconciled and a reconciling community. We will explore this reality both as a given in the New Testament and as a contemporary challenge for us today.

The New Testament Witness: The Struggle to be a Reconciled Community

Frequently we may entertain an idyllic picture of the early Church of the New Testament. There is some foundation for this in the occasional idealized portraits of church life, for example, as Saint Luke describes the early Jerusalem community in Acts of the Apostles 2:42–47 where he writes, "All who believed were together and had all things in common" (Acts of the Apostles 2:44).

When we focus on such descriptions, we may overlook the numerous references to the struggles the early Christian communities had in trying to be reconciled within themselves. Take, for example, these words of Paul to the Church in Colossae:

> As God's chosen ones, holy and beloved, clothe yourselves with compassion, kindness, humility, meekness, and patience. Bear with one another and, if anyone has a complaint against another, forgive each other; just as the Lord has forgiven you, so you also must forgive. COLOSSIANS 3:12–13

This passage indicates a task and a challenge for the Church that begins at its very beginnings. The Church is to make deliberate decisions to embrace a path of reconciliation and forgiveness within the community. The basis for this intentional style of relating to each other is the reality and experience of the Lord's forgiveness given to those who have been baptized: "[J]ust as the Lord has forgiven you, so you also must forgive" (Colossians 3:13).

The Colossians were not the only ones struggling to hold together, to be a reconciled community. Think of the Church in Corinth to whom Paul wrote:

> Now I appeal to you, brothers and sisters, by the name of our Lord Jesus Christ, that all of you be in agreement and that there be no divisions among you, but that you be united in the same mind and the same purpose. For it has been reported to me . . . that there are quarrels among you. I CORINTHIANS 1:10–11

Later, in that same letter, Paul also wrote:

> When you come together as a church, I hear that there are divisions among you.
> I CORINTHIANS 11:18

The Gospels assume that the internal reconciliation of the church community is an ongoing challenge and inescapable feature of life together. Chapter 18 of Matthew's Gospel speaks clearly to a conflicted community about how it ought to embrace reconciliation and forgiveness. He writes, "If another member of the church sins against you . . ." (Matthew 18:15).

In that same chapter Matthew recounts the powerful, and uniquely Matthean, parable of the unforgiving servant (see Matthew 18:21–35). In addition, many passages in the Gospels that describe the interaction of Jesus and his disciples begin with such phrases as, "What were you arguing about?" (see Mark 9:33).

The New Testament tells us that *when* we need reconciliation within the Church, not *if* we should need it, we are called to embrace a path of forgiveness and healing.

The Church Reconciled and Reconciling: Inner Identity and Outer Mission

Reconciliation in the Church is an absolutely central focus. It connects to the very graced and divine action in Jesus Christ which brought the Church into existence: "[J]ust as the Lord has forgiven you, so you also must forgive" (Colossians 3:13).

Reconciliation also means living out the Church's eucharistic existence which calls us and strengthens our unity as the body of Christ: "Because there is one bread, we who are many are one body, for we all partake of the one bread" (1 Corinthians 10:17). In short, the Church cannot be true to itself and its Lord without an active commitment and engagement of reconciliation within its internal life. The inner mystery of the Church demands that believers pay constant attention to being reconciled among themselves, and that the Church be a reconciled community.

At the same time, the outer mission and ministry of the Church calls for the Church to be a reconciling community in the world. The great commission at the end of Matthew's Gospel pushes the Church out into the world to make reconciled disciples of all the nations (see Matthew 28:16–20).

In the same Gospel, Jesus names those who are merciful or peacemakers or absorbed by the demands of righteousness and justice as truly blessed (see Matthew 5:3–10). In fact, the unified and reconciled life of the disciples of Jesus is the fundamental witness in and to the world that leads to faith: ". . . so that they may all be one, as you, Father, are in me and I in you, that they also may be in us, *that the world may believe that you sent me*" (John 17:21 [italics added]). The loving and reconciled relationships among disciples offer transparent witness to their discipleship: "This is how all will know that you are my disciples, if you have love for one another" (John 13:35).

Both the inner life of the Church, its mystery, and the outer life of the Church, its mission, demand that it attend to its identity and task as a reconciled and reconciling community.

Today's Challenges

Travel, communications, economic interdependence, the specter of war and terrorism, and the recognition of limited planetary resources have all shrunk the world. Differences, divisions, and even enmities that we might have ignored in the past now face us squarely and unavoidably. The identity and the mission of the Church as a reconciled and reconciling community take on a new and urgent importance. The Second Vatican Council identified this situation at the very beginning of *Lumen gentium (The Dogmatic Constitution on the Church)*.

"[T]he Church in Christ is in the nature of sacrament—a sign and instrument, that is, of communion with God and of unity among all men— [and] sets forth . . . her own nature and universal mission. The condition of the modern world lends greater urgency to this duty of the Church; for, while men of the present day are drawn ever more closely together by social, technical and cultural bonds, it still remains for them to achieve full unity in Christ" (1).

For Reflection

How can the Church be both a reconciled and a reconciling community?

How is your parish a visible sign of reconciliation?

How and why is reconciliation a public affair?

Symbol and Ritual in the Preparation for Sacraments

The *General Directory for Catechesis* refers to liturgical catechesis as an "eminent kind of catechesis." According to the *Directory*, liturgical catechesis prepares for the sacraments by promoting a deeper understanding and experience of the liturgy. [Liturgical catechesis] explains the contents of the prayers, the meaning of the signs and gestures, educates to active participation, contemplation and silence. GDC 71

Calling to mind another assertion stated in the *Directory* helps us to appreciate more fully what the *Directory* is suggesting in this key paragraph. The *Directory* describes the baptismal catechumenate as the "inspiration" and the "model" of all catechesis in the Church (see GDC 90).

The Use of Ritual in Faith Formation

The *Rite of Christian Initiation of Adults* (RCIA) spells out in detail an elaborate pastoral vision of how the catechumenate is to prepare those seeking to celebrate the sacraments of Christian initiation: Baptism, Confirmation, and Eucharist. One of the key insights embodied in that vision is the formative power of ritual experience.

The RCIA takes seriously the ancient tradition of the Church that the liturgy itself is the primary "school of faith" for those who wish to participate in the life of the Church. In its introduction to the "Period of the Catechumenate," it states that throughout the period of the catechumenate candidates and catechumens should participate in rituals that will help form them in faith and that will prepare them for full participation in the Church's sacramental life following their initiation (see RCIA 75).

Just as the RCIA itself contains directions about how to adapt its procedures for use with children of catechetical age, so the *Directory* in paragraphs 90 and 91 suggests that sacramental preparation in other contexts ought not only to draw inspiration from but also to adapt the faith-formation strategies contained in the RCIA.

RCL's *Reconciliation* program incorporates this wisdom into its catechetical approach. Each lesson contains suggested rituals for use with the children preparing to celebrate Reconciliation. These rituals are meant to be carefully integrated into the catechetical process so that they form an experiential basis for the other kinds of learning suggested elsewhere in each lesson.

Experts from the social sciences have long studied the importance of rituals in human growth and development, from early infancy right on through our most senior years. Through symbol and ritual we receive our earliest and most basic religious categories.

Our religious imagination is formed with deep and lasting impressions long before formal schooling begins. Lifelong religious values are instilled, as imperceptibly yet inexorably, as are the rest of our cultural values. Those who study how the cognitive and affective dimensions of our lives are integrated into our personality suggest that ritual and symbol play a privileged role in this process.

There is a fullness of meaning communicated through symbol and ritual, and that fullness is unequaled in its power as an agent of religious formation. The holistic nature of ritual experience makes it the ideal medium for the work of faith formation.

The Use of Symbols in Liturgical Celebrations

Because the rituals and symbols we use with children are so powerful, it is of the utmost importance that they be consistent with the message of faith we are trying to instill in the children.

One of the major reasons the Church exercises such vigilance over her liturgical rituals is the fact that they are so powerfully formative of faith. A famous line from a document of the U.S. bishops on music and liturgy put it this way: "Good celebrations foster and nourish faith. Poor celebrations may weaken and destroy it" (*Music in Catholic Worship* 6).

You will find that the choice of symbols and the ritual forms that are used in the celebrations that are provided in RCL's *Reconciliation* program have been chosen carefully and follow the lead of the Church's official liturgy. The primary symbols associated with our liturgical tradition have been selected rather than spurious, secondary symbols that sometimes are used in catechetical rituals under the guise of making these rituals more relevant to the children's experience.

There is nothing more relevant than the primal symbols and ritual forms of the liturgy. They are rooted in our deepest traditions. The meanings associated with them over centuries of use have been passed down from generation to generation as among the most precious treasures in our heritage of faith.

The rites provided in RCL's *Reconciliation* program need not be slavishly followed. In fact, it is likely that adapting them to fit the situation of particular children will often be necessary or, at least, will improve their celebration. Often in the choice of music, the arrangement of the space, even the sequence of different ritual elements, the catechist will need to make adjustments to enhance the experience for the children.

It should be noted that not every adaptation may be a good one. The suggested rituals and symbols have been very thoughtfully crafted, and are based on long experience with the Church's liturgy. These rituals try to follow basic structures and forms as a way of introducing children to the fuller and more elaborate rites they will be asked to participate in as members of the larger worshiping community.

We do a disservice to children by offering them rites that have been simplified in a manner that makes the rites quite foreign to what the children will encounter when they worship with the adult community. Rites celebrated by children should never be so different from those rites celebrated by the rest of the parish community that the children experience the sacred liturgy as unfamiliar and inaccessible.

The purpose of liturgical catechesis, as the *General Directory for Catechesis* states, is to promote a love for the liturgy and to prepare those who are catechized to participate in the Church's rites and symbols with deeper understanding (see GDC 71). A careful celebration of the rituals provided in RCL's *Reconciliation* program, together with the liturgical catechesis that accompanies them, will help initiate the children into that "full, conscious and active participation" in the liturgy that is called for in virtually all of the documents of the liturgical renewal.

For Reflection

What is your experience of ritual and symbol?

Why do the *General Directory for Catechesis* and the *Rite of Christian Initiation of Adults* place emphasis on ritual and symbol during the preparation for sacraments?

How does your parish community evaluate its liturgical celebrations?

Frequently Asked Questions

What does the Church ask of parents in sacrament preparation?

The Church views the role of parents in the religious formation of children as both a privilege and an obligation. When you presented your child to the Church for Baptism, you were distinctly reminded that you have the responsibility "to bring [your child] up in the practice of the faith" (*Rite of Baptism of Children* 56). This privilege and obligation extend to sacrament preparation.

How does my child's *Reconciliation* book include the family?

The child's *Reconciliation* book includes a "Together as a Family" section on the Scripture and doctrine pages in each chapter. In addition, an entire page is devoted to "Together as a Family" at the conclusion of each chapter. This page includes four parts:

- "Remembering Together," which invites you to share what your child has learned as well as stories of your own faith.

- "Sharing Together," which provides suggestions for family activities.

- "Praying Together," which offers a simple prayer for your family to pray together.

- "Getting Ready Together," which gives practical suggestions of ways your family can prepare for first Reconciliation together.

What does my child need to know?

My child needs to know—

- what the difference is between right and wrong.

- that accidents or mistakes are not sins.

- that when we deliberately choose to do what is wrong and turn away from God, we sin.

- that God is loving and merciful and will always forgive us if we ask.

- that Jesus has given us the sacrament of Reconciliation through which our sins are forgiven and we receive the grace to live as God's children.

- that as God forgives us we must be willing to forgive others.

How can I tell if my child is ready for first Reconciliation?

There are many indicators of readiness for first Reconciliation, most of which are intangible. As a parent, listen carefully to what your child says about wrongdoing and misbehavior. Encourage your child to take responsibility for his or her behavior rather than blaming others. Watch to see if your child is capable of being sorry and asking forgiveness of others without your prompting. Then, ask yourself the following:

- Is prayer a part of my child's life?

- Does my child have the capacity for sincere sorrow and make an honest effort to do better?

• Can my child express sorrow and describe wrongdoing in his or her own words?

How can I encourage my child's participation in the sacrament of Reconciliation beyond "first" Reconciliation?

• Plan a family party to celebrate your child's first Reconciliation. By acknowledging the importance of your child's first Reconciliation, you convey its value into the future.

• During this time of preparation, talk with your child about what constitutes a sin. Continue such conversations as your child grows older. Initiate discussions about the temptations in your child's life. How can those temptations be addressed? As your child grows into adolescence she or he will be faced with many decisions and temptations and will need your guidance in making good choices and avoiding sin.

• As a family, plan to participate in parish celebrations of Reconciliation during Lent and Advent each year. If families make this a serious commitment and plan ahead, even teenagers can arrange their schedules accordingly.

• Reflect on your own attitude toward this sacrament. As a parent, if you participate in the sacrament of Reconciliation, your child will most likely want to do so as well.

Using the *Reconciliation* Music CD

Children are engaged through all their senses, and preparation for the sacraments should be rich in sensory stimulation. Children are drawn into the spiritual environment through the visual richness of religious images and their senses. They are engaged through the light of candles, through the smell of incense, through the touch of a peace greeting or a blessing, and through the sounds of music as they listen and as they sing.

The *Reconciliation* music CD is an integral part of RCL's *Reconciliation* program. It is comprised of eighteen songs with vocals. The lyrics for these songs can be found in the *Reconciliation Catechist Guide* on pages 116–20. In addition, the CD provides the instrumental version without lyrics of eleven of the songs.

These are a few of the many ways you might use this music CD:

- Listen to all the music. If you find selections that you will include in the sacrament celebration, plan to incorporate that music into your preparation sessions. This will allow the children to become familiar with the songs.

- Use the instrumental selections as background music as the children gather for the opening prayer ritual, during a period of reflection, or while the children are completing tasks. Listening to the instrumental version of a song will help the children become familiar with the melody of a song that they will be singing at some later time.

- Encourage the children to sing songs from memory. Young children do not do well if they have to read the words to a song as they sing. Worship aids or papers with lyrics printed on them are usually more of a distraction than a help to children.

- Invite the children to sing the refrain or antiphon of a song. Have a cantor sing the verses rather than expecting the children to memorize all the verses.

- Use song refrains and antiphons as acclamations or responses. These songs on the *Reconciliation* music CD are particularly suited for this:
    —Song 7: "Envía Tu Espíritu"
    —Song 8: "Jesus, Come to Us"
    —Song 12: "Give Me a New Heart"
    —Song 13: "I'm Sorry"
    —Song 14: "Lo siento"
    —Song 15: "God of Mercy"
    —Song 16: "Be with Me, Lord"
    —Song 17: "Open My Eyes"

- Use music, either instrumental or sung, to gather for prayer. These songs on the CD are appropriate as gathering songs for the sacrament celebrations:
    —Song 1: "Like a Shepherd"
    —Song 8: "Jesus, Come to Us"
    —Song 11: "Change Our Hearts"
    —Song 17: "Open My Eyes"

- These songs are appropriate to be sung during the celebration of Reconciliation. They can also be used with the children in a variety of settings:
    —Song 5: "Pescador de Hombres"
        ("Lord, You Have Come")
    —Song 6: "I Have Loved You"

Use music abundantly as you prepare the children for first Reconciliation. Words connected to music—sung prayer—allow the children to remember and express words of praise, petition, contrition, and thanks. Music enriches the sense of the sacred for children and for people of all ages.

Using RCL's "Sacraments" Web Site

Visit RCL's web site for sacraments, which is found by simply following the link titled "Sacraments" at **www.FaithFirst.com**. The "Sacraments" home page will reveal the menu of activities and options for children, young people, parents, and catechists.

RCL's "Sacraments" web site was designed to enrich and expand this program for Reconciliation. The web site provides young people the opportunity to have fun and engage in interactive multimedia that connect to their immediate sacrament preparation. The web site gives parents the opportunity to explore further their role with their children in sacrament preparation, and it supports catechists with additional resources.

Here are some things you will find on the RCL "Sacraments" web site:

For Children and Young People
- Interactive Church Tour
- Interactive Walk Through the Rites of Reconciliation
- Games
- Fun Reviews

For Parents
- Scripture Stories
- Lectionary Connection for Each Week
- Mealtime Prayers
- Frequently Asked Questions
- Ways to Use and Expand "Together as a Family" Sections

For Catechists
- Scripture Stories
- Lectionary Connection for Each Week
- Downloads: What Difference Does It Make?
- Community Service Ideas

Here are some ways to encourage people to use the web site:

- Remind parents to go to RCL's "Sacraments" web site; provide the address at every meeting.
- Visit the web site yourself and pick out your favorite activity and share it with parents and catechists.
- Publish the web site address in your parish bulletin, newsletter, and notices sent home to parents.
- Include RCL's web site address on all correspondence to parents and catechists.
- Demonstrate one of the interactive games or activities at a parent or catechist orientation gathering.

www.FaithFirst.com
Click on *"Sacraments"*

Checklist ✔ for the Director

Six to nine months prior to the program

- ❑ Read through the *Reconciliation Program Director's Manual*, child's book, *Reconciliation Catechist Guide*, and *Reconciliation Family Guide*.
- ❑ Decide on the type of model you will use to implement the sacrament preparation program. (See "Models for Using the RCL Sacrament Preparation Program" in part one of this manual.)
- ❑ Select the number of gatherings for the children, young people, parents, and parish adults.
- ❑ Schedule sessions and reserve facilities.
- ❑ Order catechist guides and copy catechist handouts for older children preparing for the sacrament. (See "Catechesis of Older Children" in part six of this manual.)

Three to six months prior to the program

- ❑ Recruit catechists.
- ❑ Conduct catechist orientation. (See "Orientation Session with Catechists" in part five of this manual.)
- ❑ Schedule and plan additional catechist training. (See "Catechist Training and Formation" and "Catechist Retreat" in part five of this manual.)
- ❑ Publicize program. (See part three of this manual.)
- ❑ Hold registration.
- ❑ Record baptismal certificates.
- ❑ Order children's *Reconciliation* books and family guides.

One to two months prior to the program

- ❑ Hold parent orientation. (See "Orientation Meeting with Parents" in part four of this manual.)
- ❑ Arrange for the handouts to be used by older children preparing for the sacrament to be copied. (See "Handouts for Older Children" in part six of this manual.)
- ❑ Plan for room setup and use of the church for opening rituals.

- ❑ Continue with catechist training. (See "Catechist Training and Formation" and "Catechist Retreat" in part five of this manual.)
- ❑ Make decisions regarding additional prayer celebrations and service ideas. (See "Opening Rituals for Large Groups" and "Additional Prayer Celebrations" in part two of this manual. See also RCL's "Sacraments" web site.)

During the program

- ❑ Arrange for the parish flyer to be copied and distributed during the weeks of preparation. (See "A Parish Flyer: Sacrament People" in part three of this manual.)
- ❑ Coordinate the use of the blessings with the pastor and presider for use each week at the parish liturgy. (See "Parish Blessings" in part three of this manual.)
- ❑ Use the bulletin announcements each week to communicate with families in the program as well as the parish assembly. (See "Bulletin Announcements" in part three of this manual.)
- ❑ Coordinate with liturgy planners to insert weekly general intercession prayers. (See "General Intercessions" in part three of this manual.)
- ❑ Prepare and conduct sessions with children, parents, and families. (See "Parent and Child Sessions" in part four of this manual.)
- ❑ Coordinate the celebration of the sacrament with the parish team. (See "Guidelines for Planning the Celebration of the Sacraments" in part one and "Tips for Presiders" in part two of this manual.)
- ❑ Conduct retreat and practice for the celebration of the sacrament. (See "Catechist Retreat" in part five and "Celebrating Reconciliation" in part four of this manual.)

After the celebration of the sacrament

- ❑ Encourage families to reflect on the experience of the sacrament. (See RCL's "Sacraments" web site.)
- ❑ Evaluate your preparation program. (See "Program Evaluation" in part one of this manual.)

© RCL • Resources for Christian Living®

Program Evaluation

For Catechists

What was most helpful to you as a catechist?

_____

_____

Did you feel as though you were well prepared? Why? Why not?

_____

_____

What was the most important thing the children learned
or experienced during this time of preparation?

_____

_____

Children were prepared for the sacrament because . . .

_____

_____

What did you enjoy the most?

_____

_____

What was the most valuable piece of this program?

_____

_____

If you could add one thing to this program, it would be . . .

_____

_____

Program Evaluation

For Parents

What was the most important thing your child learned
or experienced during this time of preparation?

_____

_____

What did your child enjoy the most?

_____

_____

What was most helpful to you as a parent?

_____

_____

What was helpful to you as a family?

_____

_____

_____

If you could change one thing about the program, what would it be?

_____

_____

_____

If you could change the schedule, what would you do?

_____

_____

_____

Program Evaluation

For the Director

After you review the evaluations from parents and catechists and reflect on the experience of implementing this sacraments program:

What was the highlight of the program for you?

_____

_____

_____

_____

_____

What worked well?

_____

_____

_____

_____

_____

What will you do differently next year?

_____

_____

_____

_____

_____

Part Two

Prayer and Ritual

About This Section

PART TWO · Prayer and Ritual

Prayer and ritual are at the heart of our faith and liturgical celebration. This program provides rich experiences of ritual and prayer using primary symbols and ritual actions in order to prepare young people for their role as full, active, conscious participants in the liturgy.

This section of the manual includes:

- **Tips for Presiders**

    —Share the article "Tips for Presiders" with the pastor and pastoral staff. Use the reflection questions at the end of the article as a way of using the article for staff development.

    —Use this article to help improve your own style of presiding at prayer.

    —Share this article with catechists. (See "Catechist Training and Formation" in part five of this manual.)

- **Opening Rituals for Large Groups**

    —Use opening rituals for a large group if your program model includes families during the preparation.

These rituals will take place as the opening for each session. They were written and intended for intergenerational groups. (See "Parent and Child Sessions" in part four of this manual.)

—Use opening rituals at regular parish family gatherings during the year.

—Use opening rituals for a large group if you want to combine several groups of children and young people only for the celebration of the opening ritual, and then have them go back with their catechist to complete the session with their smaller group.

- **Additional Prayer Celebrations**

    Two additional prayer celebrations "Forgiveness Prayer for a Children's Group" and "Forgiveness Prayer for Families" are included in this section. These prayer celebrations can be used as a culmination to the sacrament preparation time or may be used anytime during the preparation period.

Tips for Presiders

Few laypeople have had any formal training in how to preside at liturgical gatherings. Yet, more and more, there are occasions when nonordained members of the Church are being asked to lead the Christian community in prayer. As we have come to realize how important ritual experience is for a holistic catechesis, catechists are at the forefront of this development .

Ritual celebrations are integral with the children in RCL's *Reconciliation* program. Such celebrations take on an even greater importance because we are concerned with a sacramental catechesis that aims at preparing children to enter more fully into the community's liturgical life.

Presiding over Christian community prayer is a skill that is learned. Like any other skill we learn, the more we practice, the more skilled we become. There is no substitute for personal experience; but, as a matter of fact, there are certain tips we can learn from the experience of others.

What follows is a collection of tips from seasoned presiders that may be of help to those with no formal training in the art of presiding.

● **Communicate with good body language.** Most of us are so cerebral in our approach to the celebration of liturgy that we tend to devote a disproportionate amount of attention to the themes of the day and the texts we must say.

In reality, our body language speaks far more powerfully than any of the words we say. Posture, muscle tension, and facial expression, gestures that are open and expansive rather than short and choppy—these are the critical issues to which good presiders must attend. Good presiders communicate a message with their body that is congruent with the themes intended and the texts that are spoken.

● **Know the script.** There are many similarities between the world of liturgy and the performing arts. Knowing the script inside out is a key element in a great performance by an actor, a musician, or other performer. One does not improvise well until the basics are mastered.

Presiders, in the same way, must know the entire ritual, the timing that is needed in order to make it unfold smoothly, as well as their particular parts. Much as the conductor of an orchestra keeps a range of elements working together to produce a harmonious sound, so the liturgical presider must keep an eye on more than just his or her own personal cues. If the presider is fumbling with the script to see what comes next, he or she will find it difficult to monitor the overall action and to keep the participants engaged.

● **Silence is golden.** Presiders who are new at the task tend to be most concerned about speaking their parts correctly, seeing that the music is effective, and a number of other issues that tend to fill the ritual space with sound. Remember—silence is golden.

A truly effective presider knows how to lead the children (and adults) into a peaceful quiet that is filled with deep prayer. Cultivating children's capacity for contemplative quiet, in fact, is an extremely important task of ritual prayer. For example, after saying, "Let us pray," many new presiders become uneasy with more than the briefest period of silence. But allowing a deep quiet space for the kind of prayer that dwells deep within the heart is just as important as speaking the words that follow.

● **Be present.** Personal presence is one of those qualities that is difficult to define but is clearly recognizable in a presider. All of us have been in the presence of someone who is distracted, trying to seem to be attentive but, in fact, is simply not present to us. We know when someone is not truly present.

Good presiders have a strong sense of presence. They know how to be attentive, for example, to the word proclaimed, to the community's song, to the actions of the assembly and of the various ministers, and so on. The presider's staying connected, both to the community assembled for worship and to the liturgical action that is unfolding, helps everyone pray better and with more focused energy.

● **Use primal symbols.** The language of liturgy is symbol and ritual. Good presiders have a keen sense of the difference between primal symbols and secondary symbols that are contrived and lack any basis in our Christian tradition.

Pop culture, with its superficial imagery, is constantly threatening to influence our liturgical rituals with flashy enticements and symbols that are supposedly more relevant and more accessible, especially to children. It is the responsibility of the presider to insist on symbols that are primal and rooted in our deepest Judeo-Christian memory. This is particularly important in children's liturgies, where we are attempting to introduce the children to our ancient heritage of prayer and worship.

● **Let the symbols speak.** Experience has also shown that our primal symbols—for example, water, oil, bread and wine, touch, fire and light— have a power to engage. That power is literally inexhaustible, so long as we allow the symbols to speak with a full voice. This means that symbols need to be robust and full, not minimalist or diminutive. A tiny drop of water on the palm of our hand is still water. But if we wish to evoke the power of Noah's great flood or the memory of the Red Sea parting before Moses, then we must be generous in our use of that symbol.

● **Be a transparent person of prayer.** Amid one's many concerns to do the ritual and to lead the community in prayer correctly, it is all too easy to get lost and to forget that the presider must be a person of deep and transparent faith. Unless the presider is personally engaged in prayer, it is next to impossible for the community to get caught up in a true spirit of worship. The presider's being overly nervous, self-conscious, or distracted, precludes the kind of personal authenticity in prayer that invites others into a similar posture before God. Reverence is not something that can be faked. If the presider is not praying, others will know it intuitively and immediately, even if they are too young to articulate it or are not consciously aware of that lack.

For Reflection

Which tip for presiding do you find most helpful? Why?

How can these tips assist you in developing your skill as a presider?

Use each tip and rate yourself as a presider. Use the scale of 1 to 10, with 10 being the highest.

Opening Rituals for Large Groups

Blessing with Water

Large Group Ritual

In advance:

- Prepare the space for the size of your group to gather. You may be celebrating this ritual in the church or another space conducive to prayer. Make sure there is a good sound system and people will be able to see and hear during the ritual celebration.
- Prepare the parents, catechists, and assembly for the ritual action. (See below.)
- Meet with the presider. (See "Tips for Presiders" in this part of the manual.)
- Provide the reader the Scripture reading. The reader will need time to prepare the reading.

You will need:

- *Reconciliation* music CD or arrange for a musician to lead the music for the ritual
- Large bowl of water (if you do not gather at the baptismal font)
- Bible, Lectionary, or Book of the Gospels

Gathering

Welcome the assembly and invite them to become aware of God's presence with and among them. Play instrumental music or an appropriate hymn.

LEADER: Let us begin by praying the Sign of the Cross which reminds us of our baptism.

ALL: *Make the sign of the cross, saying,*
In the name of the Father,
and of the Son,
and of the Holy Spirit. Amen.

LEADER: Loving God, our Creator,
you are with us as we gather in prayer.
Open our hearts to your word.
We ask this in the name of your Son,
Jesus Christ.

ALL: Amen.

Scripture Reading

LEADER: Let us ask the Holy Spirit to help us listen to the word of God as we sign our forehead, lips, and heart with the sign of the cross.

READER: A reading from the holy gospel according to Luke.

ALL: *Reverently make the sign of the cross on their forehead, lips, and over their heart and then say,*
Glory to you, Lord.

READER: *Proclaim Luke 15:1–7. Conclude the reading, saying,*
The gospel of the Lord.

ALL: Praise to you, Lord Jesus Christ.

Ritual: Signing with Water

Play instrumental music or an appropriate hymn. Invite the families and young people to come forward to the baptismal font or bowl of water. The parent or catechist will mark the child's forehead with the sign of the cross, address them by name, and say,

PARENT: *(Name)*, you belong to Christ. In the name of the Father, and of the Son, and of the Holy Spirit.

CHILD: Amen.

Once signed, they return to their seats.

Closing Prayer

LEADER: Loving God, Creator and Father,
you call us by name; we belong to you.
We thank you for the gift of water
that reminds us that you share your life
   with us.
Help us live as children of God.
We ask this through Jesus Christ our Lord.

ALL: Amen.

Conclude the ritual with the same hymn from the ritual gathering or another appropriate song.

Large Group Ritual

Reverence for the Word of God

In advance:

- Prepare the space for the size of your group to gather. You may be celebrating these rituals in the church or another space conducive to prayer. Make sure there is a good sound system and people will be able to see and hear during the ritual celebration.
- Prepare the parents, catechists, and assembly for the ritual action. (See below.)
- Meet with the presider. (See "Tips for Presiders" in this part of the manual.)
- Provide the reader the Scripture reading. The reader will need time to prepare the reading.

You will need:

- *Reconciliation* music CD or arrange for a musician to lead the music for the ritual
- Bible, Lectionary, or Book of the Gospels

Gathering

Welcome the assembly and invite them to become aware of God's presence with and among them. Play instrumental music or an appropriate hymn.

Have the reader process into the prayer space holding the Bible (or Book of the Gospels) in their hands at about eye level. Upon arrival at the prayer area, have the reader reverently place the opened Bible on a book stand or on the altar.

LEADER: Let us begin by praying the Sign of the Cross, which reminds us of our baptism.

ALL: *Make the sign of the cross, saying,*
In the name of the Father,
and of the Son,
and of the Holy Spirit. Amen.

LEADER: God, our loving Father,
we gather around your word to us,
the Sacred Scriptures.
Prepare our minds and hearts
to listen to your word.
We ask this through Jesus Christ our Lord.

ALL: Amen.

Scripture Reading

LEADER: Let us ask the Holy Spirit to help us listen to the word of God as we sign our forehead, lips, and heart with the sign of the cross.

READER: A reading from the holy gospel according to Matthew.

ALL: *Reverently make the sign of the cross on their forehead, lips, and over their heart and then say,*
Glory to you, Lord.

READER: *Proclaim Matthew 22:34-40. Conclude the reading, saying,*
The gospel of the Lord.

ALL: Praise to you, Lord Jesus Christ.

Ritual: Reverencing the Scriptures

Play instrumental music or an appropriate hymn used for the gathering procession. Then invite the assembly to come forward to reverence the Bible (or Book of the Gospels). For example, they may touch the book, kiss the book, or genuflect before the book.

Closing Prayer

LEADER: God, our loving Father,
today we show our reverence
for your word, the Sacred Scriptures.
Send us the Holy Spirit
to help us remember and follow your word
every day.
We ask this through Jesus Christ our Lord.

ALL: Amen.

Conclude the ritual with the same hymn from the ritual gathering or another appropriate song.

Jesus, Light of the World

In advance:

- Prepare the space for the size of your group to gather. You may be celebrating this ritual in the church or another space conducive to prayer. Make sure there is a good sound system and people will be able to see and hear during the ritual celebration.
- Prepare the parents, catechists, and assembly for the ritual action. (See below.)
- Meet with the presider. (See "Tips for Presiders" in this part of the manual.)
- Provide the reader the Scripture reading. The reader will need time to prepare the reading.

You will need:

- *Reconciliation* music CD or arrange for a musician to lead the music for the ritual
- Bible, Lectionary, or Book of the Gospels
- Easter candle, or large white candle, and taper
- Several votive candles in glass holders

Gathering

Welcome the assembly and invite them to become aware of God's presence with and among them. Play instrumental music or an appropriate hymn.

LEADER: Let us begin by praying the Sign of the Cross to remind us of our baptism.

ALL: *Make the sign of the cross, saying,*
In the name of the Father,
and of the Son,
and of the Holy Spirit. Amen.

LEADER: God of goodness and mercy,
you send us the gift of the Holy Spirit.
Open our minds and hearts to the Holy Spirit,
who is our teacher and helper.
We ask this through Jesus Christ our Lord.

ALL: Amen.

Scripture Reading

LEADER: Let us ask the Holy Spirit to help us listen to the word of God as we sign our forehead, lips, and heart with the sign of the cross.

READER: A reading from the holy gospel according to Luke.

ALL: *Reverently make the sign of the cross on their forehead, lips, and over their heart and then say,* Glory to you, Lord.

READER: *Proclaim Luke 10:29–37. Conclude the reading, saying,*
The gospel of the Lord.

ALL: Praise to you, Lord Jesus Christ.

Ritual: Candle Lighting

LEADER: *Light the Easter candle, saying,*
Jesus is the Light of the World.
Remind the assembly that Jesus called us to be lights in our world. Ask the assembly to name things that the Holy Spirit can help them do to be lights in the world. For example, "Be kind to others," "Listen attentively to parents and others," and so on. After each statement have the assembly respond,

ALL: Jesus, Light of the World, help us to be lights in the world.

LEADER: *As each response is made, have a catechist or parent light a votive candle from the Easter candle, using a taper. Votive candles can be placed around the prayer area or presented to families.*

Closing Prayer

LEADER: God of goodness and mercy,
thank you for the gift of the Holy Spirit.
Send us the Holy Spirit
to help us to live as lights in the world.
We ask this through Jesus Christ our Lord.

ALL: Amen.

Conclude the celebration with the same hymn from the ritual gathering or another appropriate song.

Praying the Our Father

In advance:

● Prepare the space for the size of your group to gather. You may be celebrating this ritual in the church or another space conducive to prayer. Make sure there is a good sound system and people will be able to see and hear during the ritual celebration.

● Prepare the parents, catechists, and assembly for the ritual action. (See below.)

● Meet with the presider. (See "Tips for Presiders" in this part of the manual.)

● Provide the reader the Scripture reading. The reader will need time to prepare the reading.

You will need:

● *Reconciliation* music CD or arrange for a musician to lead the music for the ritual

● Bible, Lectionary, or Book of the Gospels

Gathering

Welcome the assembly and invite them to become aware of God's presence with and among them. Play instrumental music or an appropriate hymn.

LEADER: Let us begin as we were baptized.

ALL: *Make the sign of the cross, saying,*
In the name of the Father,
and of the Son,
and of the Holy Spirit. Amen.

LEADER: Loving God, you are our Father.
Help us to know and trust your love for us.
Open our hearts to the Holy Spirit.
We ask this through Jesus Christ our Lord.

ALL: Amen.

Scripture Reading

LEADER: Let us ask the Holy Spirit to help us listen to the word of God as we sign our forehead, lips, and heart with the sign of the cross.

READER: A reading from the holy gospel according to Luke.

ALL: *Reverently make the sign of the cross on their forehead, lips, and over their heart and then say,*
Glory to you, Lord.

READER: *Proclaim Luke 19:1–10. Conclude the reading, saying,*
The gospel of the Lord.

ALL: Praise to you, Lord Jesus Christ.

Ritual: Praying the Our Father

Invite the assembly to pray the Our Father. If you are comfortable, lead them in praying the Our Father by slightly extending your arms and holding the palms of your hands upward. Share that this is a sign that we are opening our hearts to God's mercy and love. An alternative would be to teach the assembly simple hand gestures and pray the Our Father together, using both words and movement.

LEADER: As a sign of our unity and that we are children of God, let us pray together the prayer that Jesus taught us.

ALL: Our Father, who art in heaven,
hallowed be thy name; thy kingdom come;
thy will be done on earth as it is in heaven.
Give us this day our daily bread;
and forgive us our trespasses
as we forgive those who trespass against us;
and lead us not into temptation,
but deliver us from evil. Amen.

Closing Prayer

LEADER: God, loving Father, we gather today
to remember your great love for us.
Send us the Holy Spirit.
Help us both to forgive and seek forgiveness and to live as your children.
We ask this through Jesus Christ our Lord.

ALL: Amen.

Conclude the celebration with the same hymn from the ritual gathering or another appropriate song.

Laying On of Hands

In advance:

- Prepare the space for the size of your group to gather. You may be celebrating these rituals in the church or another space conducive to prayer. Make sure there is a good sound system and people will be able to see and hear during the ritual celebration.
- Prepare the parents, catechists, and assembly for the ritual action. (See below.)
- Meet with the presider. (See "Tips for Presiders" in this part of the manual.)
- Provide the reader the Scripture reading. The reader will need time to prepare the reading.

You will need:

- *Reconciliation* music CD or arrange for a musician to lead the music for the ritual
- Bible, Lectionary, or Book of the Gospels

Gathering

Welcome the assembly and invite them to become aware of God's presence with and among them. Play instrumental music or an appropriate hymn.

LEADER: Let us begin as we were baptized.

ALL: *Make the sign of the cross, saying,*
In the name of the Father,
and of the Son,
and of the Holy Spirit. Amen.

LEADER: God, forgiving Father,
you sent us your Son, Jesus,
to show us how much you love us.
Send us the Holy Spirit
to help us trust your forgiveness and grace.
Open our hearts to listen to your word.
We ask this through Jesus Christ our Lord.

ALL: Amen.

Scripture Reading

LEADER: Let us ask the Holy Spirit to help us listen to the word of God as we sign our forehead, lips, and heart with the sign of the cross.

READER: A reading from the holy gospel according to Luke.

ALL: *Reverently make the sign of the cross on their forehead, lips, and over their heart and then say,* Glory to you, Lord.

READER: *Proclaim Luke 15:11–32. Conclude the reading, saying,*
The gospel of the Lord.

ALL: Praise to you, Lord Jesus Christ.

Ritual: Laying On of Hands

LEADER: *Invite the parents to turn to the children to bless them with the laying on of hands. Have the parents place their open hands on the top of the head of their child, silently pray, and conclude by saying aloud,*

PARENT: Remember that God always loves you.

CHILD: Thanks be to God.

Alternative: *If parents are not present for this ritual, have catechists placed around the sanctuary and invite the young people to come forward for the blessing and return to their seats.*

LEADER: *After the assembly has celebrated the ritual of the laying on of hands, say aloud,*
Let us now pray the prayer that Jesus taught us.

ALL: Our Father ...

Closing Prayer

LEADER: *Extend and hold your hands outward, palms down, over the assembly and pray,*
God, our forgiving Father, you always love us. Send the Holy Spirit of forgiveness upon your people. Help them to trust in your forgiving love and to share your love with others. We ask through Jesus Christ our Lord.

ALL: Amen.

Conclude the ritual with the same hymn from the ritual gathering or another appropriate song.

Sharing a Sign of Peace

In advance:

● Prepare the space for the size of your group to gather. You may be celebrating these rituals in the church or another space conducive to prayer. Make sure there is a good sound system and people will be able to see and hear during the ritual celebration.

● Prepare the parents, catechists and assembly for the ritual action. (See below.)

● Meet with the presider. (See "Tips for Presiders" in this part of the manual.)

● Provide the reader the Scripture reading. The reader will need time to prepare the reading.

You will need:

● *Reconciliation* music CD or arrange for a musician to lead the music for the ritual

● Bible, Lectionary, or Book of the Gospels

Gathering

Welcome the assembly and invite them to become aware of God's presence with and among them. Play instrumental music or an appropriate hymn.

LEADER: Let us begin by praying the Sign of the Cross to remind us of our baptism.

ALL: *Make the sign of the cross, saying,*
In the name of the Father,
and of the Son,
and of the Holy Spirit. Amen.

LEADER: God, our loving Father,
you sent us your Son, the Prince of Peace.
Help us know and share the peace that the
      Holy Spirit brings us.
Open our hearts to your word
that we may learn to live as peacemakers.
We ask this through Jesus Christ our Lord.

ALL: Amen.

Scripture Reading

LEADER: Let us ask the Holy Spirit to help us listen to the word of God as we sign our forehead, lips, and heart with the sign of the cross.

READER: A reading from the holy gospel according to John.

ALL: *Reverently make the sign of the cross on their forehead, lips, and over their heart and then say,* Glory to you, Lord.

READER: *Proclaim John 14:15–27 and 20:21. Conclude the reading, saying,*
The gospel of the Lord.

ALL: Praise to you, Lord Jesus Christ.

Ritual: Peace Greeting

LEADER: We are all children of God.
Let us pray as Jesus taught us.

ALL: Our Father ...

LEADER: Jesus said, "Peace I leave with you; my peace I give to you" (John 14:27). Let us share that gift of Christ's peace with one another as Jesus shares it with us.

ALL: *Share a sign of peace.*

Closing Prayer

LEADER: God, giver of peace,
you sent us Jesus, your Son,
to show us how to live in peace with you
and with one another.
Send the Holy Spirit
to help us live as peacemakers.
We ask this through Jesus Christ our Lord.

ALL: Amen.

LEADER: The Lord frees us from our sins.
Go and live in peace.

ALL: Thanks be to God.

Conclude the ritual with the same hymn from the ritual gathering or another appropriate song.

Additional Prayer Celebrations

Forgiveness Prayer for a Children's Group

Incorporate music into this prayer. You may wish to include an opening song, a gospel acclamation, vocal or instrumental music during the procession when the children present their sheep drawings, and a concluding song. Use songs from RCL's Reconciliation music CD or other music that is familiar to the children.

Gathering

Lead the children in a procession to the prayer area and have them gather around the prayer table. Invite the children to settle themselves and to become aware of God's presence.

LEADER: Let us begin as we were baptized by praying the Sign of the Cross.

ALL: *Make the sign of the cross, saying,*
In the name of the Father,
and of the Son,
and of the Holy Spirit. Amen.

LEADER: Let us pray.
Lord, our God,
you welcome us as lost children.
You rejoice at our return
as the shepherd who finds
the lost sheep rejoices.
Send us the Holy Spirit
to help us look honestly at ourselves.
Remind us that we can always
come home again.
We make our prayer in the name
of your Son, Jesus Christ.

ALL: Amen.

Liturgy of the Word

Read aloud or invite a volunteer to read aloud Luke 15:4–6 from the Bible.

ALL: *Sing an appropriate gospel acclamation.*

READER: A reading from the holy gospel according to Luke.

ALL: Glory to you, Lord.

READER: *Proclaim Luke 15:4–6. Conclude the reading, saying,*
The gospel of the Lord.

ALL: Praise to you, Lord Jesus Christ.

Alternative: *Use the Scripture play for chapter 1, "The Lost Sheep," which can be found in part five of this manual. This will allow the children to share in the proclamation of the Gospel.*

Reflection

LEADER: Let us bow our heads and tell God we are sorry for our sins.
For the times when we do not put God first in our lives and we do not pray, we say,

ALL: We are sorry, Lord.

LEADER: For the times when we do not say God's name with respect, and we do not go to Mass, we say,

ALL: We are sorry, Lord.

LEADER: For the times when we are mean or cruel or say unkind things to others, we say,

ALL: We are sorry, Lord.

LEADER: For the times when we are dishonest, when we take things that don't belong to us, or when we do not tell the truth, we say,

ALL: We are sorry, Lord.

LEADER: For the times when we refuse to forgive others and when we are troublemakers instead of peacemakers, we say,

ALL: We are sorry, Lord.

LEADER: Lord of us all,
you are the Good Shepherd
and we are your flock.
Even when we run away from you and sin,
you always come searching for us.

Ritual

LEADER: Now, as a sign that the Good Shepherd has brought us all back together where we belong, let us join hands and pray the prayer that Jesus taught us.

ALL: Our Father ...

LEADER: And now, let us exchange a sign of peace with one another to help us remember that we are peacemakers.
Invite the children to share a sign of peace with one another.

Closing Prayer

LEADER: Let us bow our heads and
ask God's blessing.
May you always be kind and caring
to one another.

ALL: Amen.

LEADER: May you always live as children of light.

ALL: Amen.

LEADER: May you go forth in the peace and love
of the Lord.

ALL: Amen.

LEADER: And may the Lord bless us all
in the name of the Father,
and of the Son,
and of the Holy Spirit.

ALL: Amen.

Forgiveness Prayer for Families

Arrange a table for prayer. Invite five readers to share in the proclamation of the Gospel.

Incorporate music into this prayer. You may wish to include an opening song and a closing song. Use songs from the RCL's Reconciliation music CD or other music that is familiar to the children.

Gathering

Gather everyone in the prayer area. Play a recording of instrumental music or an appropriate hymn. Invite everyone to settle themselves and to become aware of God's presence.

LEADER: Let us begin as we were baptized by praying the Sign of the Cross.

ALL: *Make the sign of the cross, saying,*
In the name of the Father,
and of the Son,
and of the Holy Spirit. Amen.

LEADER: Let us pray.
Loving God, we turn to you in prayer.
We come together because you invite us
    to take time out of our busy world
to put ourselves in your presence.
We ask your help and we need your forgiveness. Send us the Holy Spirit to help us look honestly at our lives and the way that we treat one another. We ask this through Jesus Christ, our Lord.

ALL: Amen.

Liturgy of the Word

Invite five readers to proclaim the gospel story "The Forgiving Father," which is based on Luke 15:11–32.

Alternative: Use the Scripture play for chapter 5 "The Forgiving Father," which can be found in part five of this manual.

The Forgiving Father

READER 1: Today we hear a story that Jesus told about a family. This family faced many of the problems we face in our families. Let us listen carefully to this story from the Gospel as recorded by Luke.
Jesus said to the people, "A man had two sons."
The younger son said to his father:

READER 2: "Father, give me the share of the estate that is coming to me."

READER 1: So the father divided up the property. Some days later this younger son collected all his belongings and went off to a distant land. There he wasted all his money on wild living. When the son had nothing left, a famine broke out in that country. So he took a job taking care of pigs. He was so hungry he would have eaten the food he was feeding the pigs. But no one offered to give him anything. Finally, the son came to his senses and said to himself:

READER 2: "How many hired hands at my father's house have more than enough to eat, and here I am starving! I will leave and return to my father and I will say to him, 'Father, I have sinned against God and against you; I no longer deserve to be called your son. Just treat me like one of your hired hands.'"

READER 1: With that the son set off for his father's house. While he was still a long way off, his father caught sight of him and ran to greet him. He threw his arms around his son's neck and kissed him. The son said to him:

READER 2: "Father, I have sinned against God and against you. I no longer deserve to be called your son."

READER 1: The father said to his servants:

READER 3: "Quick, bring out the finest robe and put it on my son. Put a ring on his finger and shoes on his feet. Take the fatted calf and kill it. Let us eat and celebrate because my son was dead and has come back to life. He was lost and now is found."

READER 1: The celebration began. Meanwhile the elder son was out in the field. As he neared the house on his way home, he heard the sound of music and dancing. He called one of the servants and asked him the reason for the dancing and music. The servant answered:

READER 4: "Your brother is home, and your father has killed the fatted calf because he has him back home safely."

READER 1: The older son grew angry at this and he would not go in to the party. But the father came out and began to plead with him. The older son said to his father in reply:

READER 5: "For years now I have slaved for you. I never disobeyed one of your orders. Yet you never even gave me a party for my friends. Then, when my brother returns after wasting all your property, you kill the fatted calf for him and have a party."

READER 3: "My son, you are with me always, and everything I have is yours. But we must celebrate and rejoice. Your brother was dead and has come back to life. He was lost and now he is found."

READER 1: The gospel of the Lord.

ALL: Praise to you, Lord Jesus Christ.

Prayer of Sorrow

LEADER: Let us bow our heads and tell God we are sorry for our sins.
For the times when we do not put God first in our lives and we do not go to Mass, we say,

ALL: We are sorry, Lord.

LEADER: For the times when we do not say God's name with respect and we do not pray, we say,

ALL: We are sorry, Lord.

LEADER: For the times when we are mean or cruel or say unkind things to one another, we say,

ALL: We are sorry, Lord.

LEADER: For the times when we are dishonest, when we take things that don't belong to us, or when we do not tell the truth, we say,

ALL: We are sorry, Lord.

LEADER: For the times when we refuse to forgive others and when we are troublemakers instead of peacemakers in our family, we say,

ALL: We are sorry, Lord.

LEADER: Lord of us all,
you are our forgiving Father.
Even when we run away from you and sin,
you always welcome us back.
As a sign of our return to you,
let us join hands
and pray the prayer that Jesus taught us.

ALL: Our Father . . .

LEADER: And now let us share a sign of Christ's peace with one another.
Invite everyone to share a sign of peace with one another.

Closing Prayer

LEADER: Let us bow our heads and
ask God's blessing.
May you always be kind and caring
to one another.

ALL: Amen.

LEADER: May you always live as children of light.

ALL: Amen.

LEADER: May you go forth in the peace and love of the Lord.

ALL: Amen.

LEADER: And may the Lord bless us all
in the name of the Father,
and of the Son,
and of the Holy Spirit.

ALL: Amen.

Part Three

For the
Parish Assembly

About This Section

PART THREE • For the Parish Assembly

The whole community is responsible for initiation (see RCIA 9). This section was designed to assist the parish assembly with its essential role in sacrament preparation. Many members of the community have not had the opportunity to reflect on the meaning of sacraments in their lives as adults. Resources in this section can help facilitate a deeper awareness and experience of the sacraments.

This section includes:

● **Parish Blessings**

Each week during the preparation period, young people are called forward or are asked to stand at their place before the final blessing at the eucharistic liturgy. The presider and the entire community join in blessing them and sending them forth.

● **A Parish Flyer: Sacramental People**

—Reproduce the entire flyer and include it in your parish newsletter or bulletin each week of the preparation period.

—Consider making these flyers contemporary or local by adding suggestions which reinforce the message of the lead article for your particular parish community.

—Reproduce elements of the flyers directly into your newsletter or bulletin each week.

—Use the flyers as handouts for parents and adults at meetings.

—Mail the flyers to families each week of the preparation period along with any reminders you are mailing.

● **Bulletin Announcements**

These announcements can be placed in the bulletin each week as an update. You can add meeting times, scheduling information, and other details to make these fit your program.

● **Parish Involvement**

This piece provides a variety of suggestions to connect the parish community with those preparing for sacraments.

● **General Intercessions**

These prayers can be used at the Sunday liturgies, weekday liturgies, school liturgies, and other parish prayer experiences.

Parish Blessings

Chapter 1: We Belong to God

May the blessing of the Good Shepherd
be with you as you prepare to share in the
    sacrament of Reconciliation.
We ask this blessing through Christ our Lord.
Amen.

Chapter 2: We Follow Jesus

May the Lord guide your hearts
in the way of his love
and fill you with Christ-like patience.
We ask this blessing through Christ our Lord.
Amen.

Chapter 3: We Listen to the Holy Spirit

May the Lord open your minds and hearts
and help you choose to live as children
    of the light.
We ask this blessing through Christ our Lord.
Amen.

Chapter 4: We Are Sorry

May God fill you with his love.
May Jesus help you to live as he taught.
May the Holy Spirit give you the strength
    to ask forgiveness when you need to.
We ask this blessing through Christ our Lord.
Amen.

Chapter 5: We Are Forgiven

May God fill your heart with kindness
and the willingness to forgive others
    as he forgives you.
We ask this blessing through Christ our Lord.
Amen.

Chapter 6: We Are Peacemakers

May God help you to live as peacemakers,
and may the Holy Spirit fill your heart
    with the gift of his peace.
We ask this blessing through Christ our Lord.
Amen.

Sacramental People

We Belong to God

Baptism and the Forgiveness of Sin

Proof for the doctrine of original sin, someone once said, is as close as the sad stories in your daily newspaper. We do live in a broken world and in a fractured humanity marked by sin.

As innocent as newborns are, they, too, are affected by this fact. They are born into this sinful condition we call original sin and carry it within themselves. With time they grow up and add their personal sin to the original kind.

The first and fundamental liberation from sin comes to us in the sacrament of Baptism. This was the message of Saint Peter on the very first Pentecost. Those who heard him preach Christ risen from the dead asked him what they ought to do. Peter said, "Repent, and be baptized every one of you in the name of Jesus Christ so that your sins may be forgiven; and you will receive the gift of the Holy Spirit" (Acts of the Apostles 2:38).

Baptism joins us to Jesus Christ and makes us a part of the new creation. We become who God destined us to be: free and forgiven and belonging to him.

Faith Focus

Baptism makes us sharers in the life and love of God. We become adopted sons and daughters of God.

The Church Says . . .

Through Baptism all sins are forgiven as well as all punishment for sin. This includes original sin and all personal sins. Nothing remains to impede the entrance of those reborn of water and the Spirit into the kingdom of God." (See *Catechism of the Catholic Church*, 1263.)

Prayer

Loving God,
Creator and Father,
you call us by name.
We belong to you.
We thank you for the gift of water
that reminds us that you share your life
and love with us.
Send us the Holy Spirit
to help us live in your love.
We ask this in the name of Jesus Christ our Lord.
Amen.

For Reflection

What difference does it make in my life that I have been claimed by God?

Sacramental People

We Follow Jesus

The Great Commandment

At the beginning of the twentieth century Albert Einstein developed his theory of relativity and compressed it into an elegantly simple equation: $E = mc^2$, which means energy equals mass times the speed of light squared. That little equation has made a world of difference and ushered in the nuclear age.

In his teaching on the Great Commandment Jesus compressed and summarized the Law and the Prophets. In other words, he distilled for us the very will of God. And that has made all the difference as it continues to revolutionize the world.

The Gospel gives us the account of a lawyer who approached Jesus and asked, "Teacher, which commandment in the law is the greatest?" Jesus said to him, " 'You shall love the Lord your God with all your heart, and with all your soul, and with all your mind.' This is the greatest and first commandment. And a second is like it: 'You shall love your neighbor as yourself.' On these two commandments hang all the law and the prophets" (Matthew 22:36–40).

With quick, deft strokes Jesus reduces all the Law to a single great commandment of love. He also inextricably links and unifies our love of God and our love of neighbor—the one, whoever it may be, who is closest to us in our lives at the moment.

God is Love

Faith Focus

The Great Commandment is the summary and the heart of all the commandments.

The Church Says . . .

Love of God and of one's neighbor, then, is the first and greatest commandment. Scripture teaches us that love of God cannot be separated from love of one's neighbor. . . . It goes without saying that this is a matter of the utmost importance to men [and women] who are coming to rely more and more on each other and to a world which is becoming more unified every day."

THE PASTORAL CONSTITUTION ON THE CHURCH IN THE MODERN WORLD [GAUDIUM ET SPES] 24

For Reflection

How do I follow Jesus' word in my life?

Prayer

Loving God,
help us live as Jesus taught us.
Send us the Holy Spirit
to help us live the Great Commandment
and follow your word every day.
We ask this in the name of Jesus Christ
our Lord. Amen.

Sacramental People

We Listen to the Holy Spirit

Discernment

If you want to repair your car, you better know something about cars and how they run, so that you can figure out what to do. If you want to bake a cake, you better know something about the ingredients and their preparation, so that you can figure out what to do. Much of life, especially its problems and challenges, requires us to apply our minds to a task and figure out what to do.

There is a whole other range of life, however, that we cannot just figure out. It has to do with sin and forgiveness and hope and the basic direction of our lives. These are responsibilities that we do not simply figure out but rather discover. We learn to watch and wait. We ask for the help of God's Holy Spirit to enlighten us and enable us to make the right discovery of these deep truths. Spiritually, this type of discovery is what we call discernment, a process of sifting through our lives with God's help to discover the right direction or truth of our lives.

The help of the Holy Spirit is decisive. Saint Paul knew this and wrote about it to his beloved community in Corinth: "For the Spirit searches everything, even the depths of God. . . . We have received not the spirit of the world, but the Spirit that is from God, so that we may understand the gifts bestowed on us by God" (1 Corinthians 2:10b, 12).

Faith Focus

The Holy Spirit helps us make good decisions and put them into action.

The Church Says . . .

The word of God is the light for our path as we form our conscience. In faith and prayer we must listen to the word of God, assimilate it, and put it into practice. The Gifts of the Holy Spirit, the teaching of the Church, and the witness and advice of others assist us in this important task. (See *Catechism of the Catholic Church* 1785)

Prayer

God of goodness and mercy, thank you for sending us the gift of the Holy Spirit. We know that the Spirit is always with us. Help us live as lights in the world. We ask this in the name of Jesus Christ our Lord. Amen.

For Reflection

What do I hear when I listen to the Holy Spirit?

Sacramental People

AS MEMBERS OF THIS PARISH COMMUNITY PREPARE FOR SACRAMENTS,
WE THE FAITHFUL JOURNEY WITH THEM.

We Are Sorry

Conversion and the Sacrament of Reconciliation

When a corporation's profits are lagging, the board of directors may call in a new CEO to turn the company around. When a ball team is flagging, management may call in a new coach to turn it around. This "turning around" means doing business in a new way or playing ball with a new attitude and better teamwork.

The tradition of faith has its own "turn around" language. It is conversion. The word in the original Greek of the New Testament is *metanoia,* and it means quite literally "a turning around of mind and heart." The preaching and teaching ministry of Jesus begins and continues to return to this great theme of conversion. At the beginning of his ministry in Galilee, Jesus made it known: "The kingdom of God has come near; repent *[metanoeite],* and believe in the good news" (Mark 1:15).

The Gospel of Jesus summons us to a continuous conversion of heart: a

Turn away from sin and be faithful to the gospel.

constant turning away *from* the way of sin and the paths of death, a turning *to* a new way of living inspired by and following the pattern of Jesus' very own life. The sacrament of Reconciliation enables us to meet God, who calls us to conversion and who, at the same time, gives us the grace to turn our lives around.

Faith Focus

The prayer of sorrow, or act of contrition, and penance express both our decision and our desire to heal the harm we cause by our sins and to be reconciled with God and the Church.

The Church Says . . .

We can only approach the kingdom of Christ by *metanoia.* This is a profound change of the whole person by which we begin to consider, judge, and arrange our life according to the holiness and love of God, made manifest in his Son in the last days and given to us in abundance."

POPE PAUL VI,
THE APOSTOLIC CONSTITUTION
RECONCILIATION ET PAENITEMINI

For Reflection

Where in my life is there a need for conversion?

Prayer

God of mercy and forgiveness,
you invite us to leave the darkness of sin
and live in the light of your love.
Send us the Holy Spirit.
Help us that we might forgive others
as you forgive us.
We ask this in the name of Jesus Christ
our Lord. Amen.

Sacramental People

We Are Forgiven

Paths of Forgiveness and the Sacrament of Forgiveness

There are a thousand ways to say "I love you" to one another, and certainly an equal number of ways to say "I'm sorry." We seek forgiveness from one another and from God in many different ways.

In our tradition the three great personal forms of seeking God's forgiveness have been prayer, fasting, and almsgiving (or supporting the poor). We can add to these other practices, such as praying a specific prayer of contrition, doing some good deed or act of charity for someone in need, and making peace with those whom we have offended or who have offended us.

More than a personal or subjective plea for forgiveness, the sacrament of Reconciliation is a particular path of assured forgiveness. God has entrusted his forgiving and healing power to the Church. If we do what is required of us—namely, are contrite or sorry, confess our sins, receive absolution, and do our penance—we are assured that God's forgiveness has touched our lives. God makes his forgiveness tangible, objective, and assured in this sacrament. In the case of serious sin, which we are obligated to confess at least once a year, this assurance of forgiveness is of the greatest importance.

Faith Focus

In the sacrament of Reconciliation God forgives our sins through the ministry of bishops and priests.

The Church Says . . .

The people of God accomplish and perfect this continual repentance in many different ways. They share in the sufferings of Christ by enduring their own difficulties, carry out works of mercy and charity, and adopt ever more fully the outlook of the Gospel message. Thus the people of God become in the world a sign of conversion to God. All this the Church expresses in its life and celebrates in its liturgy."

RITE OF PENANCE 4

For Reflection

What difference does it make that I have asked for forgiveness and have been willing to forgive?

Prayer

God, our forgiving Father,
you always love us.
Send us the Holy Spirit of forgiveness.
Help us trust in your forgiving love.
Help us share your forgiving love with others.
We ask this in the name of Jesus Christ
our Lord. Amen.

Sacramental People

We Are Peacemakers

Peacemakers in the Twenty-first Century

Jesus taught, "Blessed are the peacemakers, for they will be called children of God" (Matthew 5:9). Often we stand before these words perplexed, motionless, not knowing what to do. The conflicts of our times, whether played out in the world at large or in our society or even within our families, seem to be too much to deal with. We would like to make peace, but we do not know how.

The first step is to meet and know Jesus Christ "for he is our peace" (Ephesians 2:14). This encounter happens in God's word and in the sacrament of Reconciliation. We come to know him and how he reconciled us with God and with one another through his cross (see Ephesians 2:16). In Christ we come to know the way of peace.

Another critical step is to take our experience of Jesus, our peace, and begin to listen to others, to make offers of reconciliation, and to lend support to the works of justice that lay a foundation for peace. Then the words of James will ring true: "And a harvest of righteousness is sown in peace for those who make peace" (James 3:18).

Faith Focus

In the sacrament of Reconciliation God makes us sharers in God's gift of peace and renews our calling to share that peace with others.

The Church Says . . .

In the climate of increased cultural and religious pluralism which is expected to mark the society of the new millennium, it is obvious that . . . dialogue will be especially important in establishing a sure basis for peace and warding off the dread specter of those wars of religion which have so often bloodied human history. The name of the one God must become increasingly what it is: *a name of peace and a summons to peace."*

POPE JOHN PAUL II IN *NOVO MILLENNIO INEUNTE* 55

For Reflection

How have I tried to live as a peacemaker?

Prayer

God, giver of peace,
you sent us Jesus, your Son,
to show us how to live in peace with you
    and with one another.
Send the Holy Spirit
to help us live as peacemakers.
We ask this in the name of Jesus Christ
    our Lord. Amen.

Bulletin Announcements

Chapter 1

We Belong to God

This week the young people of the parish preparing for Reconciliation reflected on Baptism, which marks us as belonging to Jesus Christ, the Son of God. One of the central images the writers of Sacred Scripture used to describe God's love for his people was the image of God as the shepherd of his people. How are we as a parish helping children to grow in a deep love for God?

Chapter 2

We Follow Jesus

This week the young people of the parish preparing for Reconciliation reflected on the Great Commandment. Keeping God's commandments and living the law of love are the source and foundation of holiness. How do we as a parish live the command of Jesus to love one another as he has loved us?

Chapter 3

We Listen to the Holy Spirit

This week the young people of the parish preparing for Reconciliation reflected on the Holy Spirit who helps us make good decisions. The Holy Spirit gifts us with the courage to overcome obstacles that stand in our way of loving God and others, and with the wisdom to value God above all creatures. How do we as a parish show that the grace of the Holy Spirit is alive in us?

Chapter 4

We Are Sorry

This week the young people of the parish preparing for Reconciliation reflected on penance and the desire to heal the hurt caused by sin. Living a life in Christ demands a continuing conversion of heart, a life of penance, with hope in God's mercy and trust in his grace. How do we as a parish share in the Paschal mystery, the great mystery of Christ's love, the mystery of mercy?

Chapter 5

We Are Forgiven

This week the young people of the parish preparing for Reconciliation reflected on the story of the prodigal son and the forgiving father. Each time we pray the Our Father we are reminded of God's forgiving love and our call, as children of God, to share that forgiving love with others. How do we as a parish welcome people unconditionally with a heart filled with joy?

Chapter 6

We Are Peacemakers

The week the young people of the parish preparing for Reconciliation reflected on God's gift of peace. All the baptized are anointed to announce the kingdom and make all people sharers in the peace of Christ. We are blessed and bring God's blessings to others. How do we as a parish strive to live as peacemakers and to make a difference?

Parish Involvement

Initiating people into the Church is the responsibility of the People of God (see *Rite of Christian Initiation of Adults* 9). Invite the members of the parish community to take a role in preparing young people for the sacraments. Here are some suggestions for involving your parish:

- Invite people in the parish to become a prayer partner for one of the children preparing for the sacraments. Provide a list of the names of the children who are preparing for the sacraments. Ask a member of the parish to take the name of one child and to pray specifically for that child on a regular basis.

- Present all the children who are preparing for the sacraments to the parish. This can be done by displaying a group photograph of all the children or by introducing the group at Mass.

- Write notes and letters of encouragement to the children who are preparing for the sacraments. Make available a list of the names of the children who are preparing for the sacraments. Invite parish members to write a note to one of the children and send it to the parish office. The program director can distribute all the letters at one time. Make sure that each child receives some letters of encouragement.

- Use the general intercessions, blessings, bulletin announcements, and bulletin inserts that are found in this section of the *Reconciliation* program director's manual to inform and involve the people in the parish in the children's preparation for sacraments.

General Intercessions

The general intercessions, or prayer of the faithful, are prayers of the community. Here are some suggestions of petitions for inclusion in your parish's general intercessions during the time of sacrament preparation. Please adapt these to the liturgical celebration and make them your own.

Petitions to Accompany the Chapters in the Child's Book

Chapter 1: We Belong to God

PETITION: For the young people of the parish preparing for the sacrament of Reconciliation, that they remember always that God loves them and has called them by name. Let us pray to the Lord.

RESPONSE: Lord, hear our prayer.

Chapter 2: We Follow Jesus

PETITION: For the young people of the parish preparing for the sacrament of Reconciliation, that as they follow Jesus' Great Commandment, they discover a reverence for God and for one another. Let us pray to the Lord.

RESPONSE: Lord, hear our prayer.

Chapter 3: We Listen to the Holy Spirit

PETITION: For the young people of the parish preparing for the sacrament of Reconciliation, that they grow in their ability to listen to the Holy Spirit and allow the Holy Spirit to be their guide. Let us pray to the Lord.

RESPONSE: Lord, hear our prayer.

Chapter 4: We Are Sorry

PETITION: For the young people of the parish preparing for the sacrament of Reconciliation, that they continue to grow in their understanding of and relationship with our God of mercy and forgiveness. Let us pray to the Lord.

RESPONSE: Lord, hear our prayer.

Chapter 5: We Are Forgiven

PETITION: For the young people of the parish preparing for the sacrament of Reconciliation, that they come to know God's healing touch through celebrating this sacrament. Let us pray to the Lord.

RESPONSE: Lord, hear our prayer.

Chapter 6: We Are Peacemakers

PETITION: For the young people of the parish preparing for the sacrament of Reconciliation, that they recognize themselves as peacemakers in the world. Let us pray to the Lord.

RESPONSE: Lord, hear our prayer.

Other Petitions for Inclusion in the General Intercessions

For Parents, Families, and Catechists

PETITION: For the parents, families, and catechists
of those preparing for the sacrament
of Reconciliation, that they may witness
to God's healing forgiveness and love.
Let us pray to the Lord.

RESPONSE: Lord, hear our prayer.

For the Parish Community

PETITION: For our parish community
that we bear witness to Jesus' power
of healing and reconciliation.
Let us pray to the Lord.

RESPONSE: Lord, hear our prayer.

Part Four

For the Family

About This Section

PART FOUR · For the Family

The role of the family is woven throughout this entire program—in the child's book, in the older children handouts, in the *Reconciliation Family Guide* for parents, and in notes for parents. This part of the program director's manual supplements and further develops these resources. It includes:

- **Orientation Meeting with Parents**
  This orientation meeting can be held at the beginning of the preparation for sacraments period.

- **How to Use the** *Reconciliation Family Guide*
  —As the program director there are various ways you can incorporate the family guide into your sacrament preparation program. This piece highlights many of these ways.
  —The features and function of the family guide are described in this piece.

- **Parent and Child Sessions**
  —These sessions provide two options for family sessions: First, the parents stay with their child for the entire session; second, the parents are with their child for an opening session and a closing session with an adult-focused session held while children are in age-appropriate groupings.
  —The adult-focused sessions can be used as a parish adult formation program. Invite all interested adults to participate.
  —The adult-focused sessions can be used as a parish Lenten program focusing on updating the parish's awareness and understanding of Reconciliation.

  —The adult-focused sessions can be incorporated into a process for Catholic adults who are returning to the Church.

- **Celebrating Reconciliation**
  This section which contains both the individual rite and communal rite for reconciliation, will help families of older children understand the celebration of Reconciliation. The same section is found in the back of the child's book.

- **Examination of Conscience**
  This examination of conscience can be used during the communal celebration of Reconciliation.

- **Raising Moral Children, What Do Children Understand About Sin? and Readiness for Reconciliation**

  —These three essays make perfect handouts for parents. You can distribute these at registration, parent orientation meetings, or other parent gatherings.

  —The first two essays can be used as handouts during the year at other parenting functions. You may have a mothers' group or an active parent group at your school that would find these informative.

- **Frequently Asked Questions**
  Use this as a handout at parent orientation or anytime adults or parents are asking questions about children and the sacrament of Reconciliation.

Orientation Meeting with Parents

Purpose

- Inform the parents about sacrament preparation.

- Clarify the role of parents, catechists, the parish, and Church.

- Present the parents with an overview of the sacrament preparation program for Reconciliation.

- Invite the parents into a partnership with the parish for sacrament preparation.

Suggested Elements for the Meeting

Welcome and Opening Prayer

- Create a hospitable and nonthreatening environment.

- Welcome parents and thank them for attending.

- Open with prayer.

Opening Process Questions

Begin by inviting parents to share with one another responses to one or more of these or similar questions:

- Why do I want to hand on my faith to my child?

- What was my experience of preparing for sacraments?

- What do the sacraments mean to me?

After parents have engaged in sharing with one another, ask for a few responses to be shared with the whole group.

Outline of Orientation

- What does the Church ask of parents? What is the role as parents?

- What is the focus of preparation for the sacrament of Reconciliation?

- What are the elements of a sacrament catechesis program?

- What are the components of RCL's *Reconciliation* program?

- How does my child's *Reconciliation* book include the family?

- What is the schedule for the program and what is my commitment?

- What are some of the frequently asked questions by parents preparing their children for this sacrament?

What Does the Church ask of Parents? What is their Role as Parents?

Pope John Paul II in his 1994 Letter to Families reasserts the privileged responsibility of parents in the faith formation of their children. He writes:

> *"Parents are the first and most important educators of their own children, and they also possess a fundamental competence in this area: they are educators because they are parents* (16).

The Church views the role of parents in the religious formation of children as both a privilege and an obligation. When you presented your child to the Church for Baptism, you were distinctly reminded that you have the responsibility "to bring [your child] up in the practice of the faith" (*Rite of Baptism of Children* 56).

This obligation and privilege extend to sacrament preparation. It is important to remember that it has been within your family that your child has first come to faith. And it is within your family setting that your child will continue to practice the faith and witness the daily example of Catholic believers.

What is the Focus of Preparation for the Sacrament of Reconciliation?

The focus of preparation for the sacrament:

- is not just "first" Reconciliation. More importantly, it is preparation for a lifetime of being forgiven and healed in the sacrament of Reconciliation.

- is not only about cognitive learning (this is covered more effectively during ongoing catechesis) but especially about a period of spiritual preparation for the sacrament.

- is not about graduation or completion in any way, but a celebration of a new beginning of a lifetime living in the generosity of a gracious God.

- is about introducing young people into a life of faith and worship.

- is a way of incorporating young people into the life of Christ and into the community that lives, celebrates, and bears witness to faith in Jesus Christ.

What are the Elements of a Sacrament Catechesis Program?

Our program of preparation weaves together these essential elements for sacrament catechesis.

- Ritual experience and expression—particularly those rituals and symbols that evoke the ritual language of sacraments.

- Prayer—both communal and individual. This includes prayer within the family, within the parish assembly, within the preparation group, and private prayer with oneself.

- Sacred Scripture—particularly those passages that enlighten our understanding of the sacraments.

- Doctrine/Liturgy—particularly the Church's teachings and worship with a focus on God's love and presence in our lives, the invitation of Jesus Christ to the forgiveness of sin, and the power of the Holy Spirit that enables us to respond to God in love and prayer.

- What Difference Does This Make?—the application and integration of the ritual, prayer, Scripture, and doctrine into our life experience.

What are the components of RCL's *Reconciliation* program?

- Child's keepsake book or handouts for older children

- Catechist guide

- Family guide

- Program director's manual

- Music CD

- Web site

Encourage parents to visit RCL's "Sacraments" web site by following the link titled "Sacraments" at **www.FaithFirst.com**. There is a whole section "For Parents" on the web site to assist them during this time of sacrament preparation

How does the child's *Reconciliation* book include the family?

RCL's *Reconciliation* child's book includes a "Together as a Family" section on each of the Scripture and doctrine/liturgy pages in each chapter. In addition, each chapter concludes with an entire page devoted to "Together as a Family." This page includes four parts:

- "Remembering Together," which invites parents and children to share what they have learned as well as share their own stories of faith.

- "Sharing Together," which provides suggestions for family activities.

- "Praying Together," which offers a simple prayer for the family to pray together.

- "Getting Ready Together," which gives practical suggestions on ways the family can prepare for the celebration of the sacrament together.

The child's book also contains:

- Six core chapters

- Celebrating Reconciliation—a walk-through of the celebration of the sacrament

- Examination of Conscience

- The Ten Commandments

- The Beatitudes

- The Precepts of the Church

- My Daily Prayers

- Glossary

- Scripture Prayer Cards

- Keepsake Certificate

What is the schedule for the program and what is the parents' commitment?

Here is where you would provide parents and families with the schedule for your program—namely, the days, times—and the commitment you are expecting from them. You would also present the model of implementation along with expectations for attending sessions. Your program director's manual gives you complete outlines for parent meetings, family sessions, and suggested formats.

What are some of the frequently asked questions by parents preparing their children for this sacrament?

Copy the article "Frequently Asked Questions" found in this section of the manual and distribute it to parents. This is a great way to address concerns and questions prior to the start of your preparation program.

Family Guides

If you are using the *Reconciliation Family Guide* in your preparation program, you might want to distribute them at this gathering. See the article "How to Use the *Reconciliation Family Guide*," found in this part of the manual.

Conclusion

Invite questions

Provide parents the opportunity to ask questions.

Closing Prayer

Close the meeting with prayer. You may wish to use one of the "Sending Forth Rituals" found in the *Reconciliation Catechist Guide.*

How to Use the *Reconciliation Family Guide*

Each chapter of the *Reconciliation* child's book is processed in four easy-to-read and easy-to-use pages in the *Reconciliation Family Guide*.

Page 1: Background Essay

This brief, easy-to-read essay gives background on the faith theme that will be discussed in the chapter.

Page 2: Overview

This page presents the lesson in summary form. The main elements on this page are:

- **What We Will Learn**
  This identifies the major faith theme of the chapter.

- **What We Will Need**
  This lists the items that are needed for this lesson.

- **What We Will Do**
  This outlines clear and simple steps to process the chapter of the child's book.

- **Looking for More**
  This suggests additional resources that will enrich or extend the lesson.

Page 3: Sharing Together

This page contains a detailed explanation of the process for the parent to share the chapter with their child.

"Closing Prayer," which is found on this page, provides a short family prayer that can be used to conclude the time the family spends together.

Page 4: Family Ritual

The family ritual is essential to the lesson. The entire lesson builds upon the common prayer experience and shared reflection on the ritual.

Parent and Child Sessions

Introduction

These lesson outlines are intended for sessions that include parents and children together. The outlines can be used for all six lessons or for selected lessons. You may want to have families work individually, or you might want families to work in pairs for the parent/child portions.

The process for these lessons is best suited to a ninety-minute time period, but the time period can be adapted as your situation dictates. The percentage of time allotted to the parts of the lesson is:

Parts I and II	45 percent
Part III	35 percent
Parts IV and V	20 percent

SESSION 1 · We Belong to God

Part I **Parents and children together**
- Pray the opening prayer ritual, "Blessing with Water," which is found in part five of this manual.
- Discuss the ritual experience, using page 5 of the child's book.

Part II **Parents and children together**
- Discuss the "Faith Focus" question on page 6 of the child's book.
- Share the Scripture story "God Loves Us" on page 6 of the child's book.
- Discuss the Scripture story, using the question on page 7 of the child's book.
- Optional: If time allows, do the family activity on page 7 of the child's book.

Part III **Breakaway groups**

A. Children meet in their peer age groups.

Catechists and children complete pages 8 and 9 in the child's book. The process is outlined on pages 34 and 35 in the *Reconciliation Catechist Guide.*

B. Adults meet as a large group.

Adults read and discuss either of the following articles from this program director's manual.
- The "Sacramental People" flyer for week 1, which is found in part three of this manual.
- "Frequently Asked Questions," which is found in this section of the manual.

Part III *Alternative:* **Parents and children together**

Parents and children together complete "Step Three" on page 18 in the *Reconciliation Family Guide.*

Part IV **Parents and children together**
- Do "Together as a Family" on page 9 of the child's book.
- Complete page 10, "What Difference Does This Make in My Life?" of the child's book.
- Discuss "My Faith Choice" on page 10 of the child's book and provide time for parents and children to share their choices with one another.
- Remind the families to complete page 11, "Together as a Family," at home as preparation for next week.

Part V **Parents and children together**

Pray the "Sending Forth Ritual" for chapter 1, as found in the catechist guide on page 38.

SESSION 2 · We Follow Jesus

Part I   Parents and children together

- Pray the opening prayer ritual, "Reverence for the Word of God," which is found in part five of this manual.
- Discuss the ritual experience, using page 13 of the child's book.

Part II   Parents and children together

- Discuss the "Faith Focus" question on page 14 of the child's book.
- Share the Scripture story "The Great Commandment" on page 14 of the child's book.
- Discuss the Scripture story, using the question on page 15 of the child's book.
- Optional: If time allows, do the family activity on page 15 of the child's book.

Part III   Breakaway groups

A. Children meet in their peer age groups.

Catechists and children complete pages 16 and 17 in the child's book. The process is outlined on pages 46 and 47 in the *Reconciliation Catechist Guide.*

B. Adults meet as a large group.

Adults read and discuss either of the following articles from this program director's manual.

- The "Sacramental People" flyer for week 2, which is found in part three of this manual.
- "Raising Moral Children," which is found at the end of this section of the manual.

Part III   *Alternative:* Parents and children together

Parents and children together complete "Step Three" on page 22 in the *Reconciliation Family Guide.*

Part IV   Parents and children together

- Do "Together as a Family" on page 17 of the child's book.
- Complete page 18, "What Difference Does This Make in My Life?" of the child's book.
- Discuss "My Faith Choice" on page 18 of the child's book and provide time for parents and children to share their choices with one another.
- Remind the families to complete page 19, "Together as a Family," at home as preparation for next week.

Part V   Parents and children together

Pray the "Sending Forth Ritual " for chapter 2, as found in the catechist guide on page 50.

© RCL · Resources for Christian Living®

SESSION 3 · # We Listen to the Holy Spirit

Part I   Parents and children together

- Pray the opening prayer ritual, "Jesus, Light of the World," which is found in part five of this manual.
- Discuss the ritual experience, using page 21 of the child's book.

Part II   Parents and children together

- Discuss the "Faith Focus" question on page 22 of the child's book.
- Share the Scripture story "The Good Samaritan" on page 22 of the child's book.
- Discuss the Scripture story, using the question on page 23 of the child's book.
- Optional: If time allows, do the family activity on page 23 of the child's book.

Part III   Breakaway groups

A. Children meet in their peer age groups.

Catechists and children complete pages 24 and 25 in the child's book. The process is outlined on pages 58 and 59 in the *Reconciliation Catechist Guide.*

B. Adults meet as a large group.

Adults read and discuss either of the following articles from this program director's manual.

- The "Sacramental People" flyer for week 3, which is found in part three of this manual.
- "What Do Children Understand About Sin?" which is found at the end of this section of this manual.

Part III   *Alternative:* Parents and children together

Parents and children together complete "Step Three" on page 26 in the *Reconciliation Family Guide.*

Part IV   Parents and children together

- Do "Together as a Family" on page 25 of the child's book.
- Complete page 26, "What Difference Does This Make in My Life?" of the child's book.
- Discuss "My Faith Choice" on page 26 of the child's book and provide time for parents and children to share their choices with one another.
- Remind the families to complete page 27, "Together as a Family," at home as preparation for next week.

Part V   Parents and children together

Pray the "Sending Forth Ritual " for chapter 3, as found in the catechist guide on page 62.

SESSION 4 · We Are Sorry

Part I **Parents and children together**
- Pray the opening prayer ritual, "Praying the Our Father," which is found in part five of this manual.
- Discuss the ritual experience, using page 29 of the child's book.

Part II **Parents and children together**
- Discuss the "Faith Focus" question on page 30 of the child's book.
- Share the Scripture story "Zacchaeus" on page 30 of the child's book.
- Discuss the Scripture story, using the question on page 31 of the child's book.
- Optional: If time allows, do the family activity on page 31 of the child's book.

Part III **Breakaway groups**

A. Children meet in their peer age groups.

Catechists and children complete pages 32 and 33 in the child's book. The process is outlined on pages 70 and 71 in the *Reconciliation Catechist Guide.*

B. Adults meet as a large group.

Adults read and discuss either of the following articles from this program director's manual.

- The "Sacramental People" flyer for week 4, which is found in part three of this manual.
- "Learning the History: The Essential Parts of the Sacrament," which is found in part one of this manual.

Part III *Alternative:* **Parents and children together**

Parents and children together complete "Step Three" on page 30 in the *Reconciliation Family Guide.*

Part IV **Parents and children together**
- Do "Together as a Family" on page 33 of the child's book.
- Complete page 34, "What Difference Does This Make in My Life?" of the child's book.
- Discuss "My Faith Choice" on page 34 of the child's book and provide time for parents and children to share their choices with one another.
- Remind the families to complete page 35, "Together as a Family," at home as preparation for next week.

Part V **Parents and children together**

Pray the "Sending Forth Ritual" for chapter 4, as found in the catechist guide on page 74.

SESSION 5 · We Are Forgiven

Part I **Parents and children together**

- Pray the opening prayer ritual, "Laying On of Hands," which is found in part five of this manual.
- Discuss the ritual experience, using page 37 of the child's book.

Part II **Parents and children together**

- Discuss the "Faith Focus" question on page 38 of the child's book.
- Share the Scripture story "The Forgiving Father" on page 38 of the child's book.
- Discuss the Scripture story, using the question on page 39 of the child's book.
- Optional: If time allows, do the family activity on page 39 of the child's book.

Part III **Breakaway groups**

A. Children meet in their peer age groups.

Catechists and children complete pages 40 and 41 in the child's book. The process is outlined on pages 82 and 83 in the *Reconciliation Catechist Guide.*

B. Adults meet as a large group.

Adults read and discuss either of the following articles from this program director's manual.

- The "Sacramental People" flyer for week 5, which is found in part three of this manual.
- "An 'Uninterrupted Task': Continuing Conversion and Conscience Formation," which is found in part one of this manual.

Part III ***Alternative:* Parents and children together**

Parents and children together complete "Step Three" on page 34 in the *Reconciliation Family Guide.*

Part IV **Parents and children together**

- Do "Together as a Family" on page 41 of the child's book.
- Complete page 42, "What Difference Does This Make in My Life?" of the child's book.
- Discuss "My Faith Choice" on page 42 of the child's book and provide time for parents and children to share their choices with one another.
- Remind the families to complete page 43, "Together as a Family," at home as preparation for next week.

Part V **Parents and children together**

Pray the "Sending Forth Ritual" for chapter 5, as found in the catechist guide on page 86.

SESSION 6 · We Are Peacemakers

Part I **Parents and children together**

- Pray the opening prayer ritual, "Sharing a Sign of Peace," which is found in part five of this manual.
- Discuss the ritual experience, using page 45 of the child's book.

Part II **Parents and children together**

- Discuss the "Faith Focus" question on page 46 of the child's book.
- Share the Scripture story "The Gift of Peace" on page 46 of the child's book.
- Discuss the Scripture story, using the question on page 47 of the child's book.
- Optional: If time allows, do the family activity on page 47 of the child's book.

Part III **Breakaway groups**

A. Children meet in their peer age groups.

Catechists and children complete pages 48 and 49 in the child's book. The process is outlined on pages 94 and 95 in the *Reconciliation Catechist Guide*.

B. Adults meet as a large group.

Adults read and discuss either of the following articles from this program director's manual.

- The "Sacramental People" flyer for week 6, which is found in part three of this manual.
- "Sin and Grace," which is found in part one of this manual.

Part III *Alternative:* **Parents and children together**

Parents and children together complete "Step Three" on page 38 in the *Reconciliation Family Guide*.

Part IV **Parents and children together**

- Do "Together as a Family" on page 49 of the child's book.
- Complete page 50, "What Difference Does This Make in My Life?" of the child's book.
- Discuss "My Faith Choice" on page 50 of the child's book and provide time for parents and children to share their choices with one another.
- Remind the families to complete page 51, "Together as a Family," at home.

Part V **Parents and children together**

Pray the "Sending Forth Ritual" for chapter 6, as found in the catechist guide on page 98.

Celebrating Reconciliation

Jesus gave us the sacraments. Christ is present in the Church and acting in the sacraments. The sacraments make us sharers in the life and love of God. They make us one with God and with our church family. We receive grace to live holy lives as children of God and followers of Jesus.

The sacrament of Reconciliation is one of the sacraments Jesus gave the Church. After he was raised from the dead, Jesus gave the apostles the gift of the Holy Spirit and the power to forgive sins (John 20:21–23). The Church does this work today through the power of the Holy Spirit and the ministry of bishops and priests. One important way they do this is in the sacrament of Reconciliation.

Here are two ways we can take part in the celebration of the sacrament of Reconciliation.

The Individual Rite for Reconciliation

Examination of Conscience

We prepare ourselves to celebrate this sacrament. Before we meet with the priest, we examine our conscience. We spend time praying. We ask the Holy Spirit to help us know how we have failed to live as children of God and followers of Jesus.

Examining our conscience helps us to name our sins and to tell God we are sorry. There is a list of questions on page 64 of the child's *Reconciliation* book that will help you examine your conscience.

GREETING

The priest greets us. Together we pray the Sign of the Cross.

> **Priest and penitent:** In the name of the Father,
> and of the Son,
> and of the Holy Spirit. Amen.

Next, the priest reminds us how much God loves us.
The priest may pray, using these or similar words:

> **Priest:** May God, who has enlightened
> every heart,
> help you to know your sins and trust
> in his mercy.
>
> **Penitent:** Amen.

READING THE WORD OF GOD

The priest may read a story from the Bible to us or welcome us with words from the Bible. The Bible is the story of God's love and mercy. When we listen to the Bible, we are listening to God's own word to us. God is telling us that he always loves us. He is telling us what it means to be a child of God. Here is a story the priest might read to you.

A man had two sons. The younger son said to his father, "Father, give me my share of our family's money." So the father divided his money between his two sons. The younger son left home. He went off to live by himself. Soon the son wasted all his money. He had no money to buy food.

The son became very hungry. The son was very sorry and decided to return home. The father saw the son walking toward their home. He ran to his son and held him in his arms. The son said to his father, "Father, I am sorry." The father was very happy to have his son home again.   BASED ON LUKE 15:11–32

CONFESSION OF SINS AND ACCEPTANCE OF A PENANCE

Confession of Sins

We tell our sins to the priest. The priest will never tell anyone the sins we confess to him. When we confess our sins, we show that we trust that God always loves us. We show we care about our friendship with God. We must confess mortal sins. We may also confess venial sins.

Acceptance of Our Penance

After we confess our sins, the priest talks to us. He names some of the ways we can live a holy life. He gives us a penance. A penance is something we do or say that shows we are sorry for and want to make up for our sins. Our penance helps us to repair or heal the harm we have caused by our sins. We accept and promise to do the penance. We say or do our penance as soon as possible after celebrating the sacrament. When we are truly sorry for our sins, we want to make up, or be reconciled, with God and with the Church. We want to live as Jesus taught us.

PRAYER OF SORROW AND ABSOLUTION

Prayer of Sorrow

We pray a prayer of sorrow. Our prayer of sorrow is called an act of contrition. This shows we are truly sorry for our sins. We can pray this form of the act of contrition or we can pray one of the other prayers of sorrow the Church gives us (see "My Daily Prayers," page 71 of the child's book). Or we can also use our own words.

My God,
I am sorry for my sins with all my heart.
In choosing to do wrong
and failing to do good,
I have sinned against you
whom I should love above all things.
I firmly intend, with your help,
to do penance, to sin no more,
and to avoid whatever leads me to sin.
Our Savior Jesus Christ suffered and died for us.
In his name, my God, have mercy.

Absolution

Jesus gave the apostles the ministry, or work, to forgive sins. Bishops and priests share in that same work. God forgives us our sins through the words and actions of the priest in the sacrament of Reconciliation. The priest extends his hands over our head or places his hands on our head as he prays:

Priest: God, the Father of mercies,
           through the death and resurrection
               of his Son
           has reconciled the world to himself
           and sent the Holy Spirit among us
           for the forgiveness of sins;
           through the ministry of the Church
           may God give you pardon and peace,

The priest makes the sign of the cross over our head as he says:

> and I absolve you from your sins
> in the name of the Father,
> and of the Son, †
> and of the Holy Spirit.

Penitent: **Amen.**

Our Amen shows that we believe that God has forgiven our sins. We are made one again, or reconciled, with God and with our church family.

PRAISE OF GOD AND DISMISSAL

Praise of God

God forgives us as the father in the Bible story forgave his younger son. Together with the priest we praise God.

Priest: Give thanks to the Lord,
for he is good.

Penitent: **His mercy endures**
for ever.

Dismissal

The priest sends us forth. He says these or similar words:

Priest: Go in peace,
and proclaim to the world
the wonderful works of God
who has brought you
salvation.

We are children of God. We want to tell everyone about God's love. We share God's gift of peace with our family, friends, and neighbors. We are peacemakers.

The Communal Rite for Reconciliation

We can celebrate this sacrament with other members of our church family. Together we listen to the word of God. We listen to the story of God's love for us. We are invited to conversion, or to live as Jesus taught us. We examine our conscience. We take a careful look at how we are living as children of God and followers of Jesus. We help each other through prayer.

INTRODUCTORY RITES

Song

We gather as the community of the Church. As the priests, readers, and other ministers enter, we stand. We sing a hymn about forgiveness or peace. We remember how much God loves us.

> **All:** **Hear us, Lord,**
> **for you are merciful and kind.**
> **In your great compassion,**
> **look on us with love.**

Greeting

The priest greets us. His words remind us that the Holy Spirit and God's grace invite us to be sorry for our sins and to celebrate this sacrament. He welcomes us with these or similar words:

> **Priest:** **Grace, mercy, and peace**
> **be with you from God the Father and**
> **Christ Jesus our Savior.**
>
> **All:** **And also with you.**

Opening Prayer

The priest invites us to pray. He uses these or similar words:

Priest: Brothers and sisters, God calls us to conversion; let us therefore ask him for the grace of sincere repentance.

We pray in silence for a few minutes. Then the priest prays aloud.

Priest: Lord,
hear the prayers of those who call on you,
forgive the sins of those who confess to you,
and in your merciful love
give us your pardon and your peace.
We ask this through Christ our Lord.

All: Amen.

CELEBRATION OF THE WORD OF GOD

We listen attentively to the Bible, the word of God. There may be several readings. There is always a reading from the Gospel. As we listen to the readings, the Holy Spirit invites us to think about God's love and mercy and to be sorry for our sins.

First Reading

We sit and listen to a story about God's love and mercy from the Old Testament. The reader concludes, saying,

Reader: The word of the Lord.

All: Thanks be to God.

Psalm Response

We show that we trust God and his love and mercy by singing or saying several verses of a psalm. For example:

Reader: All my hope, O Lord, is in your loving kindness.

All: All my hope,
O Lord, is in
your loving kindness.

Second Reading

We remain seated and listen again as God tells us about his love and mercy. This reading is from the New Testament, but not from the Gospels. The reader concludes, saying,

> Reader: The word of the Lord.
>
> All: Thanks be to God.

Alleluia or Gospel Acclamation

Jesus is present with us. We stand and greet Jesus, who speaks to us in the Gospel. For example, we sing or say,

> All: Alleluia.

Gospel

Jesus tells us about God's mercy and love for us. He shows us the way to live as children of God and peacemakers. The priest begins,

> Priest: A reading from the holy gospel according to (name of Gospel writer).

The priest concludes by saying,

> Priest: The gospel of the Lord.
>
> All: Praise to you, Lord Jesus Christ.

Homily

The priest helps us to think about what God's word is saying to us.

Examination of Conscience

We think about how we are living as children of God. We ask the Holy Spirit to help us to be sorry for our sins and to give us the courage to live as Jesus taught us.

RITE OF RECONCILIATION

Expressing Our Sorrow Together

Together, as God's people, we respond to the Holy Spirit. We express our sorrow for our sins to God and one another. We use these or similar words:

All: **I confess to almighty God,**
and to you, my brothers and sisters,
that I have sinned through my own fault
in my thoughts and in my words,
in what I have done,
and in what I have failed to do;
and I ask blessed Mary, ever virgin,
all the angels and saints,
and you, my brothers and sisters,
to pray for me to the Lord our God.

Next, we stand and pray a litany of contrition or sing a song. Then we pray the Lord's Prayer. Jesus often told us about his love for his Father and God the Father's love for us. In this prayer, we call God "Father" as Jesus invited us to do. We tell God the Father how much we love him. We ask him for the grace we need to live as children of God.

Priest: **Let us now pray to God our Father in the**
words Christ gave us, and ask him for his
forgiveness and protection from all evil.

All: **Our Father . . .**

Individual Confession and Absolution

We then go individually to the priest to confess our sins. The priest gives us a penance. We say or do our penance as soon as possible after celebrating the sacrament. Doing the penance is a sign that we want to change our lives. We want to repair, or heal, the harm we have caused by our sins. Then the priest, in the name of God, absolves us, or frees us, from our sins. The priest extends his hands over our head or places his hands on our head as he prays:

Priest: God, the Father of mercies,
           through the death and
                resurrection of his Son
           has reconciled the world to himself
           and sent the Holy Spirit among us
           for the forgiveness of sins;
           through the ministry of the Church
           may God give you pardon and peace,

He makes the sign of the cross over our head as he says:

           and I absolve you from your sins
           in the name of the Father,
           and of the Son, †
           and of the Holy Spirit.

Penitent: Amen.

Proclamation of Praise for God's Mercy

We have been reconciled with God and with our church family. Our friendship with God and one another has been made stronger. We sing a psalm or hymn or say a litany praising God for his mercy. For example:

Reader: The Lord is loving and kind:
           his mercy is for ever.

All: **The Lord is loving and kind:**
           his mercy is for ever.

Reader: Worship the Lord with gladness;
           come to his presence with singing.

All: **The Lord is loving and kind:**
           his mercy is for ever.

Reader: Know that the Lord is God.
           It is he that made us, and we are his.

All: **The Lord is loving and kind:**
           his mercy is for ever.

PSALM 100:2–3

Concluding Prayer of Thanksgiving

Together we give thanks to God. The priest leads us in prayer, using these or similar words:

Priest: All-holy Father,
           you have shown us your mercy
           and made us a new creation
           in the likeness of your Son.
           Make us living signs of your love
           for the whole world to see.
           We ask this through Christ our Lord.

All: **Amen.**

CONCLUDING RITE

Blessing and Dismissal

The sacrament of Reconciliation has changed us. God has given us the grace of his forgiveness. He has strengthened our friendship with him and with one another. Before we leave, the priest asks God to bless us. He asks God to give us the grace to live as children of God.

Priest: May the Lord guide your
        hearts in the way of his love and fill
    you with Christ-like patience.

All: **Amen.**

Priest: May he give you strength
    to walk in newness of life
    and to please him in all things.

All: **Amen.**

Priest: May almighty God bless you,
    the Father,
    and the Son, †
    and the Holy Spirit.

All: **Amen.**

The priest sends us forth. He says these or similar words:

Priest: The Lord has freed you from your sins.
    Go in peace.

All: **Thanks be to God.**

We are children of God. We want to tell everyone about God's love. We share God's gift of peace with our family, friends, and neighbors. We are peacemakers.

Song

We may sing a closing song praising and thanking God for his gift of forgiveness.

Examination of Conscience

We examine our conscience to help us live as children of God and followers of Jesus. We ask ourselves how well we are living or not living as Jesus taught us. We think about the Ten Commandments, the Beatitudes, and what the Church teaches us. We can ask ourselves questions like these:

- How am I showing or failing to show my love and respect for God?
    - —Do I spend time with God in prayer? Do I listen reverently to God's word at Mass?
    - —Do I speak God's name or Jesus' name respectfully? Or have I spoken God's name or Jesus' name inappropriately when I was angry or to impress my friends?

- How am I showing or failing to show my love and respect for other people and for myself?
    - —Do I respect my parents, teachers, and others who have the responsibility to care for me? Do I cooperate with them and obey them?
    - —Do I care for my health and follow safety rules?
    - —Do I treat other people fairly and with kindness? Or have I been mean to others?
    - —Am I generous? Do I share what I have with others, especially people in need? Or have I been greedy?
    - —Am I truthful? Or have I lied to get out of trouble or to get someone else into trouble?

Raising Moral Children

Parents often wonder why some children seem to have an innate moral compass, while others lack any sense of morality. Why does this happen? Is there some foolproof formula for raising moral children? The good news is—there are many ways that parents can shape the morality of their children. The bad news is—when it comes to raising children, nothing is foolproof!

Even if children are well behaved, honest, truthful, and respectful, they may not yet be moral—they may simply be obedient. So how do we help children to become moral individuals? How can we move from seeking obedience to building morality?

First of all, in order to become moral people, we must recognize our connection to God, to others, to our place in the larger community. If we are unable to relate to God and to others, we care only for ourselves. How, then, can a parent help their child to develop as a moral person?

As with so much of human development, moral development grows over many years and begins with one's developing sense of being connected to other people. From birth, an infant's relationship to others is based on need. An infant needs to be fed, warm, and dry; and other people will fulfill those needs. Early in life, a baby relates to family members from this basis of need.

The first step into an unselfish connection to another is when we invite a toddler to share a toy. It is in this family setting that children become sharing individuals who can relate to others without biting, pushing, pulling hair, or hitting.

In early childhood the ability to choose begins to develop. Toddlers love to choose the clothing they will wear and the foods they will eat. While these choices may sometimes be bothersome to a parent, it is these first choices that lay the foundation for later, more critical choices the child will make.

As children advance in age, they begin to develop their ability to make decisions. Whether sound or flawed, it is these early decision-making attempts that prepare children for the significant decisions they will be called upon to make in the future. Gradually, children develop confidence in their own ability to make good choices.

By the time children are in the middle grades, they are developing the ability to predict the results of their behavior. This means that a child can logically predict the outcomes of particular actions. Although this is an important piece of moral development, it can be problematic for children since they seldom stop to think before they act. This difficulty continues even into adolescence and beyond.

Moral development is a gradual and a lifelong process. Here are some ways that parents can nurture their child's moral growth:

- Help your child develop genuine care and concern for other people both within your family and in the broader community. Foster both the ability to get along with other people and the traits of being a good friend.

- Help your child make good choices. Do not rescind the privilege of choosing in the wake of a poor choice. Simply suggest that your child make a better choice.

- Always affirm good decisions your child makes.

- Remind your child often to stop and think before acting.

- When your child does something wrong, take the time to discuss the situation without anger. Help your child see some of the ways a better choice or decision might have been made and the wrongdoing avoided.

- Be an example of what it means to live as a moral person.

What Do Children Understand About Sin?

In the early years of our children's lives, parents struggle to help them learn the difference between right and wrong. Later, as children approach the age for first Reconciliation, the time comes to speak with them about sin.

When we speak about sin with our children, we first need to clarify one important issue: All that is wrong is not necessarily sinful. It is wrong for children to neglect to do their homework or their chores, but such neglectful behavior is seldom sinful. However aggravating these decisions may be, parents need to be careful not to speak of these actions as sins. For the most part, these wrong behaviors of childhood are simply part of the process of becoming a responsible person.

Likewise, accidents and mistakes are not sins. It is not uncommon for young children to confuse their accidents and mistakes with sinful behavior. Therefore, parents need to help children realize that sin is a deliberate act to choose something that we know is wrong. A mistake or an accident, even when it has harmful consequences, is not a sin.

Sin is something entirely apart from the petty wrongdoings and annoying mistakes that occur in the day-to-day life of childhood. It is good to remember that sin is always a *deliberate* action.

In order for an action to be sinful there are four requirements:

1. It must be a sin.

2. You must know it is a sin.

3. You must stop, think, and decide to commit the sin. This is what we often refer to as *adequate reflection*.

4. You must act to commit the sin; in other words, make a deliberate choice to sin.

These four conditions are required for sin, whether you are an adult or a child.

Young children may also have difficulty recognizing what qualifies a particular sin as serious. Primary grade children usually base their judgment of serious sin on two things: First, if the sinful action involves a large quantity or volume of something, a child will think the sin qualifies as serious. Second, the child takes a cue from the parent's reaction. If a parent gets very angry or upset over something, the child logically concludes that it must be serious. Fortunately, as children grow older, they develop a more appropriate yardstick for measuring the seriousness of sins.

Another confusing element for children as they progress in their development is the idea of intent. Children often struggle to understand this concept because it is so abstract. Parents can help children understand the concept of intent by using some simple examples. For example: If you miss Sunday Mass because you are ill, it is not a sin. It was not your intent to miss Mass since, were it not for your illness, you would be at Mass. However, if you skip Sunday Mass in order to watch a football game, it is a sin. It is your deliberate intent to miss Mass. You may also find it helpful, as you speak with children about wrongdoing, to simply ask them, "What exactly did you intend when you acted in that way?"

It is very important to remember that parents and children need to have a continuing dialogue on temptation, wrongdoing, and sin. This is not a conversation that happens only around the time of first Reconciliation. This conversation needs to be an ongoing conversation, a discussion that continues through adolescence. A parent might initiate such a conversation by asking opening questions such as:

- How can you tell when you've done something wrong?

- How can you tell when wrongdoing is sinful or serious?

- What are the temptations in your life?

Home is where children learn about right and wrong. Parents are responsible for teaching children how to deal with the temptations of life. As children grow, their understanding of sin changes, and parents need to maintain a strong presence in the lives of their children if they are to influence the behaviors and values of their children.

Readiness for Reconciliation

Whether a child preparing for Reconciliation is seven, eight, or nine years old, that child is only capable of age-appropriate readiness. A seven-year-old can only understand God's mercy and forgiveness as a seven-year-old. Furthermore, the child's ability to comprehend such concepts as conscience, temptation, intention, and sin—both mortal and venial—is also limited by age and moral development. As the child grows in knowledge and faith, his or her understanding and appreciation of the sacrament of Reconciliation will naturally deepen.

The moral development of children

Moral development occurs gradually over many years, and it is difficult to predict with precision just when particular moral stages will occur. With that caution, we offer these generalizations. They are simply guidelines that will help you gain some insight into and appreciation of the moral development of your child:

- Prior to the age of eight or nine, children may have difficulty distinguishing between mistakes they have made, what has occurred accidentally, and what they have willfully done.

- Prior to the age of eight or nine, children have two standards for determining when sin is serious, or mortal. One standard is the intensity of the adult reaction to the event. The other is the quantity or volume involved; for example, the greater the number of items stolen (as opposed to the value of the items), the more serious the sin.

- The intention to do wrong—which is essential to sinful action—is often beyond a child's understanding. Children will eventually realize that they must *intend* to act sinfully in order for their act to be a sin.

- Because of the very nature of children, children often do not think before they act. When a child says, "I didn't mean to do it," they are probably telling the truth. They simply did not stop to think. Adults need to remind children often to stop and think before they act.

- Parents can help their children reflect on their actions by calmly asking their children such questions as: Why did you do that? What did you think would happen? Did you realize what you were doing was wrong or sinful? Did you intend to act sinfully? What can you do to keep from doing this again?

What are reasonable expectations for a child's readiness for the sacrament?

There are several indicators that point to your child's readiness for the sacrament. In the discernment of a child's readiness, it is reasonable to expect that:

- the child has been participating in Sunday Mass on a regular basis.

- the child has been participating in ongoing catechesis and will continue to do so.

- prayer is a part of the child's life and is experienced within the family as well as within the Church.

© RCL • Resources for Christian Living®

- the child can recognize the difference between right and wrong.

- the child knows the difference between accidents or mistakes and freely choosing a sinful behavior.

- the child understands what constitutes mortal and venial sin.

- the child has the capacity for sincere sorrow and can make an honest effort to do better.

- the child understands that God will always forgive us—all we need to do is ask.

- Jesus has given us the sacrament of Reconciliation through which our sins are forgiven and we receive the grace to live as God's children.

- we must be willing to forgive others, as God forgives us.

Dioceses and parishes may vary in their readiness requirements for children approaching the sacrament of Reconciliation for the first time. Whatever the standard of readiness your diocese and parish has established, be certain that your child is not led to believe that he or she has to earn the privilege of sharing in God's mercy and forgiveness in the sacrament of Reconciliation. God's mercy and forgiveness can never be earned; they are God's gifts to us.

Frequently Asked Questions

What does the Church ask of parents in sacrament preparation?

The Church views the role of parents in the religious formation of children as both a privilege and an obligation. When you presented your child to the Church for Baptism, you were distinctly reminded that you have the responsibility "to bring [your child] up in the practice of the faith" (*Rite of Baptism of Children* 56). This privilege and obligation extend to sacrament preparation.

How does my child's *Reconciliation* book include the family?

The child's *Reconciliation* book includes a "Together as a Family" section on the Scripture and doctrine pages in each chapter. In addition, an entire page is devoted to "Together as a Family" at the conclusion of each chapter. This page includes four parts:

- "Remembering Together," which invites you to discuss what your child has learned as well as to share stories of your own faith.

- "Sharing Together," which provides suggestions for family activities.

- "Praying Together," which offers a simple prayer for your family to pray together.

- "Getting Ready Together," which gives practical suggestions for ways your family can prepare for first Reconciliation together.

What does my child need to know?

Your child needs to know—

- the difference between right and wrong.

- that accidents or mistakes are not sins.

- that when we deliberately choose to do what is wrong and turn away from God, we sin.

- that God is loving and merciful and will always forgive us if we are sorry and ask.

- that Jesus has given us the sacrament of Reconciliation through which our sins are forgiven and we receive the grace to live as God's children.

- that we must be willing to forgive others as God forgives us.

How can I tell if my child is ready for first Reconciliation?

There are many indicators of readiness for first Reconciliation, most of which are intangible. As a parent, listen carefully to what your child says about wrongdoing and misbehavior. Encourage your child to take responsibility for his or her behavior rather than blaming others. Watch to see if your child is capable of being sorry and of asking forgiveness of others without your prompting. Then ask yourself the following:

- Is prayer a part of my child's life?

- Does my child have the capacity for sincere sorrow, and does he or she make an honest effort to do better?

- Can my child express sorrow and describe wrongdoing in his or her own words?

How can I encourage my child's participation in the sacrament of Reconciliation beyond "first" Reconciliation?

- Plan a family party to celebrate your child's first Reconciliation. By acknowledging the importance of your child's first Reconciliation, you convey the value of celebrating this sacrament into the future.

- During this time of preparation, talk with your child about what constitutes a sin. Continue these conversations as your child grows older. Initiate discussions about the temptations in your child's life and how those temptations might be addressed. As your child grows into adolescence he or she will be faced with many decisions and temptations and your child will need your guidance to help him or her make good choices and avoid sin.

- As a family, plan to participate in parish celebrations of Reconciliation during Lent and Advent each year. If you make this a serious commitment and plan ahead, even your teenagers can arrange their schedules accordingly.

- Reflect on your own attitude toward this sacrament. As a parent, if you participate in the sacrament of Reconciliation, your child will most likely want to do so as well.

Part Five

For the
Catechist

About This Section

PART FIVE • For the Catechist

The catechist is the person who will work closely with those preparing for the sacraments. Catechists themselves must be people of faith who echo the spirit of Jesus in what they say as well as who they are.

This section includes:

- **Orientation Session with Catechists**
  This session can be used immediately following the recruitment of catechists and prior to the beginning of the sacrament preparation program.

- **Catechist Training and Formation**
  These ideas for further training and formation of catechists can be implemented in a variety of settings throughout the year.

- **Catechist Retreat**
  —The retreat will place the formation and training of your catechists in the context of a spiritual retreat setting.
  —The retreat can be adapted and used during Lent with any group of adults.

- **Scripture Plays**
  These plays can be used in place of the Scripture reading during the opening prayer rituals or during the Scripture section of the child's session.

- **Opening Rituals from the Catechist Guide**
  —Even though these rituals are in the catechist guide, you may want to have a copy of them if you are the presider for the opening ritual.
  —These rituals can be copied in order to facilitate the celebration of the opening prayer rituals with the entire group participating in the program.

Orientation Session with Catechists

Opening Prayer Ritual

Laying On of Hands

Gathering

Gather the catechists around the baptismal font in the church. Invite the catechists to center themselves and to become aware of God's presence within and among them.

Alternative: *Play a recording of instrumental music or an appropriate hymn. Gather the catechists in the prayer area. Invite the catechists to center themselves and to become aware of God's presence within and among them.*

LEADER: Let us begin as we were baptized.

ALL: *Making the sign of the cross, say,*
In the name of the Father,
and of the Son,
and of the Holy Spirit. Amen.

LEADER: God, our forgiving Father,
Jesus showed us how much you love us.
Send us the Holy Spirit
to help us trust your forgiveness
  and grace.
Open our hearts to listen to your word.
We ask this in the name of Jesus Christ
  our Lord.

ALL: Amen.

Scripture Reading

LEADER: Let us make the sign of the cross on our forehead, lips, and over our heart and ask the Holy Spirit to help us listen to the word of God.

READER: A reading from the holy gospel according to Luke.

ALL: *Reverently make the sign of the cross on their forehead, lips, and over their heart and then say,*
Glory to you, Lord.

READER: *Proclaim Luke 15:11–32. Conclude the reading, saying,*
The gospel of the Lord.

ALL: Praise to you, Lord Jesus Christ.

Ritual: Laying On of Hands

LEADER: *Invite the catechists to come forward one at a time. Place your open hands on the head of each catechist and silently pray. Conclude each prayer by saying aloud,*
Remember that God always loves you.

After you have imposed your hands on each catechist's head and prayed silently, all respond,

ALL: Thanks be to God.

LEADER: *After you have completed this ritual with each catechist, say,*
Let us now pray the prayer Jesus taught us.

ALL: Our Father . . .

Closing

LEADER: *Hold your hands outward, palms down and extended over the catechists, and pray,*
God, our forgiving Father,
you always love us.
Send the Holy Spirit of forgiveness
  upon these catechists.
Help them trust in your forgiving love.
Help them share your forgiving love
  with others.
We ask this in the name of Jesus Christ
  our Lord.

ALL: Amen.

Reflection on the Ritual

After the opening ritual ask the catechists the following questions, one at a time. After each question listen and draw out all responses.

- What was it like for you to experience this ritual?

- What symbols/actions touched you?

- What does this ritual experience say to you about God? Jesus? The Holy Spirit? The Church?

Next explain:

You just experienced the first piece of the sacrament preparation program you will be using at the beginning of each chapter. Through the experience of the opening ritual, you will be preparing the way for meaningful celebration of the sacraments. By helping the children and families discover Scripture, Tradition, doctrine, liturgy, and share together as a family you will also assist your group to prepare for a lifetime of celebrating sacraments in the Church.

Presentation and Discussion

What is the focus of preparation for the sacrament of Reconciliation?

Distribute copies of the Reconciliation Catechist Guide. *Refer to the front matter in the guide when reviewing the following information.*

The focus of preparation for the sacraments is not:

- just for "first" Reconciliation, but, more importantly, it is a preparation for a lifetime of being forgiven and healed in the sacrament of Reconciliation.

- not only about cognitive learning (this is covered more effectively during ongoing catechesis); but more significantly, it is a period of spiritual preparation.

- about graduation or completion in any way, but it is a celebration of a new beginning of a lifetime living in the generosity of a gracious God.

The focus of preparation for the sacraments is:

- about introducing young people into a life of faith and worship.

- a way of incorporating young people into life in Christ and into the community that lives, celebrates, and bears witness to faith in Jesus Christ.

What is the role of the catechist?

The role of the catechist in sacrament preparation is one of teacher and spiritual guide, or companion on the journey. The catechist will create the environment that facilitates the young people to experience the love of God through Jesus Christ. The real challenge for the catechist is to help the young people experience Jesus in their heart.

What are the guiding principles of this sacrament program?

RCL's *Reconciliation* sacrament preparation program weaves together important elements for sacrament catechesis. These elements are:

- Ritual experience and expression—particularly those rituals and symbols that evoke the ritual language of the sacraments.

- Prayer—both communal and individual, including prayer within the family, within the parish assembly, and within the preparation group.

- Sacred Scripture—particularly those passages that enlighten our understanding of the sacraments.

- Doctrine—particularly those beliefs on God's love and merciful presence in our lives, on the power of the Holy Spirit who enables us to respond to God in love and prayer, and on Jesus' example of the forgiveness of others.

● What Difference Does This Make?—the application and integration of ritual, prayer, Scripture, and doctrine into our life.

How do the lessons work?

Have the catechists turn to the first chapter in their guide as you walk them through the steps in the lesson.

Step One: Ritual Celebration—The session begins with a ritual celebration using primary symbols, ritual actions, and the proclamation of Scripture. After the opening ritual celebration, the young people reflect on the ritual action and its connection to their lives and to the sacramental life of the Church.

Step Two: Scripture—The Scripture proclaimed in the ritual is read again as part of the young people's lesson. The young people are invited into the story and helped not only to understand the story but to see their life experience in light of the Scripture story.

Step Three: Doctrine/Liturgy—The Church's teachings regarding the sacraments flow out of the opening ritual and Scripture and are presented along with the liturgical, or sacramental, component that celebrates the doctrine.

Step Four: What Difference Does This Make?—In this step of the catechetical process, the ritual, Scripture, and doctrine all come together. The young people integrate what they are learning into their lives. They are invited to live what they have learned and to put their faith into practice.

Step Five: Together as a Family—The family connection is a strong component throughout this program. Each step of the above process includes the family. The "Together as a Family" page, which concludes each chapter, invites families to integrate what they have learned into the life of the family by providing families the opportunity to remember,

share, pray, and get ready for the celebration of Eucharist. There are also other family aspects to this program. It is up to you to decide how your parish/school will be implementing these family dimensions of the program.

What are the components of RCL's *Reconciliation* program?

Have copies of each component available to show the catechists.

● Child's keepsake book or handouts for older children

● Catechist guide

● Family guide

● Program director's manual

● Music CD

● Web site—follow the link titled "Sacraments" at **www.FaithFirst.com**.

How will this program be used in your parish or school? What is the catechist's commitment?

Here is where you would provide catechists with the schedule for the program—the days and times, and the commitment you are expecting. The model of implementation would be presented along with any expectations for the catechists' participation in catechist training and formation. This program director's manual gives you complete outlines for catechist training, educational handouts, and so on.

Frequently Asked Questions

You may wish to copy the article "Frequently Asked Questions" found in part one of this manual. This is a great way to address the concerns and questions that the catechists might have prior to beginning the actual preparation program.

Invite Questions

End with an opportunity for the catechists to ask any questions or for a clarification of any information they have heard. Invite them to read through their guide and get back with you if they should have any further questions.

Closing Prayer

Play a recording of an instrumental version of an appropriate song from the Reconciliation *music CD. Then invite the catechists to gather in the prayer area or around a table where the children's books and program materials are displayed.*

LEADER: All holy Father,
you have given us new life in Jesus,
    your Son.
Send the Holy Spirit
to strengthen us to be
living signs of your love for everyone
    to see.

ALL: Amen.

LEADER: Bow your heads and ask
    for God's blessing.
May God, the Father, the Son,
    and the Holy Spirit,
help you live as Jesus taught.

ALL: Amen.

LEADER: May God fill your heart with kindness
to forgive others as he forgives you.

ALL: Amen.

LEADER: May almighty God bless you,
the Father,
and the Son,
and the Holy Spirit.

ALL: Amen.

LEADER: *Conclude by saying,*
With these resources,
may you be empowered
to teach and witness the
    presence of Jesus.
Go in peace to love and serve the Lord.

ALL: Thanks be to God.

Invite each catechist to take the appropriate materials for their group, such as children's books, handouts for older children, music CD, and so on.

Catechist Training and Formation

Using *Echoes of Faith*
"Catholic Morality" Module

- Schedule four one-hour weekly training sessions or one four-hour session on a Saturday morning or afternoon.

- Secure the *Echoes of Faith* video "Catholic Morality." Order a participant booklet for each catechist. Follow the process for the *Echoes of Faith* program that is outlined on the "Preface" page of the participant booklet.

- This module will give the catechists a background into the theology, the teachings of the Church, and the practice of Catholic morality. It will provide the catechists sound background as they begin to prepare others for the sacrament of Reconciliation.

Note: Echoes of Faith, produced by RCL Resources for Christian Living, is a project of the National Conference for Catechetical Leadership (NCCL). It is the most widely used catechist/teacher formation program in North America. This 13-module series includes a companion booklet for each participant with learning design, articles, reflection questions, and prayers. There is a director's manual that contains flexible formation models for numerous settings. It is available by calling RCL customer service at 877-275-4725.

Using the Professional Articles in
RCL's *Reconciliation Program Director's Manual*

The professional articles in RCL's *Reconciliation Program Director's Manual* may be copied and distributed for use as follows:

- Have the catechists read the articles individually.

- Schedule several short gatherings for the catechists to come together and discuss the articles, using the discussion questions found at the end of each article. Set aside several fifteen-minute sharing experiences over the course of several weeks.

Catechist Retreat

This retreat model uses the professional articles found in this manual as a source of reflection during the retreat experience. This format can be adapted to an evening of reflection if such an adaptation better fits the particular needs of your program schedule.

Each participant will need a copy of the articles "The Paths of Forgiveness: The Many Ways God's Forgiveness Touches Our Lives" and "Sin and Grace," a Bible, a journal, and a pen or pencil.

Outline for the Retreat

- Welcoming
- Opening prayer ritual
- Reflecting on the ritual experience
- Alone time: Reading of the article, personal reflection time
- Sharing with a partner: Each person will be paired off with a sharing partner.
- Sharing in large group: Reflection and sharing
- Closing Prayer

Welcoming

The retreat may take place at a retreat or conference center or at the parish hall or school facility. Make sure the environment is conducive for prayer and reflection. Try to eliminate any distractions that would take away from the reflective mood of the day.

Play instrumental music as people gather. You may wish to serve light refreshments.

Opening Prayer Ritual

Gathering

Gather the catechists in the church or the chapel or in a prayer area. Invite the catechists to center themselves and to become aware of God's presence within and among them.

LEADER: Let us begin as we were baptized.

ALL: *Make the sign of the cross, saying,*
In the name of the Father,
and of the Son,
and of the Holy Spirit. Amen.

LEADER: God, forgiving Father,
Jesus showed us how much you love us.
Help us trust in your forgiveness
and grace.
Open our hearts and minds to listen
and to be transformed by your word.
We ask this through Jesus Christ
our Lord.

ALL: Amen.

Scripture Reading

LEADER: Let us make the sign of the cross on our forehead, lips, and over our heart and ask the Holy Spirit to help us listen to the word of God.

READER: A reading from the holy gospel according to Luke.

ALL: *Reverently make the sign of the cross on their forehead, lips, and over their heart and then say,*
Glory to you, Lord.

READER: *Proclaim Luke 15:11–32. Conclude the reading, saying,*
The gospel of the Lord.

ALL: Praise to you, Lord Jesus Christ.

Reflection

LEADER: *Ask the group to silently reflect on the word of God in their hearts. After a minute or two of silent reflection, invite the catechists to share their reflections on the word of God.*

Prayers of Intercession

Conclude the reflection with intercessory prayer.

LEADER: Let us pray to God who cares for all, and say,

ALL: Lord, hear our prayer.

LEADER: For our world,
that violence, division, and strife cease.

ALL: Lord, hear our prayer

LEADER: For leaders of all nations,
that they may be guided by a deep sense of justice in all their deliberations.

ALL: Lord, hear our prayer.

LEADER: For the Church,
that we may be faithful to the demands of the Gospel.

ALL: Lord, hear our prayer.

LEADER: For the poor, the hungry, the homeless, those who have lost hope,
that through us they may experience God's healing presence.

ALL: Lord, hear our prayer.

LEADER: And for what else shall we pray. *(Pause.)*
Let us join these prayers into one with the prayer Jesus gave us.

ALL: Our Father . . .

Ritual: Laying On of Hands

LEADER: *Invite the catechists to come forward one at a time. Place your open hands reverently on the head of each person, and pray silently. Conclude each prayer by saying aloud,*
Remember, God's love is always with you.

ALL: Thanks be to God.

LEADER: *After you have completed the ritual action with each catechist, invite everyone to prayer, saying aloud,*
Let us pray.
Extend your hands outward, palms down over the catechists, and continue to pray,
God, our forgiving Father,
you always love us.
Send your Holy Spirit of forgiveness upon these catechists.
Help them trust in your forgiving love.
Help them share your forgiveness with others.
We ask this in the name of Jesus Christ our Lord.

ALL: Amen.

Reflecting on the Ritual Experience

After celebrating the ritual, ask the catechists the following questions, one at a time. After each question listen and draw out all responses.

● What was it like for you to experience this ritual?

● What symbols or actions touched you?

● What does this experience say to you about God? Jesus? The Holy Spirit? The Church?

Alone Time

Distribute to each catechist copies of the articles "The Paths of Forgiveness: The Many Ways God's Forgiveness Touches Our Lives" and "Sin and Grace," which are found in part one of this manual. Invite the catechists to find a private place to read through the articles, highlight or write notes on the articles, and respond to the reflection questions at the end of the articles. Decide on an appropriate time to meet back with the group.

Sharing with a Partner

Once everyone has returned, invite each catechist to join with a partner and share responses to the reflection questions.

Sharing in a Large Group

After sufficient time for each pair of catechists to discuss the reflection questions, invite people to share their responses to the articles and questions with the entire group. Ask the following questions:

- What insights and learning did you glean from your own reflection?

- What insights and learning did you glean from listening to others?

- How have these articles assisted in broadening or affirming your understanding of God's forgiveness?

Alone Time

Once again provide the catechist time for personal reflection. Invite them to reflect on these questions:

- How does God's forgiveness make a difference in my life?

- How does God's forgiveness make a difference in the life of the Church?

Sharing in a Large Group

After allowing sufficient time for each catechist to reflect on the questions, gather the entire group together and ask the catechists to share a word, phrase, or image that describes how God's forgiveness makes a difference.

Point out the reflection questions listed in the *Reconciliation Catechist Guide* at the conclusion of the "Background" essay on the first page of each chapter. Encourage them to reflect and journal, using those questions as they prepare to teach each chapter.

Closing Prayer

LEADER: All-holy Father,
you have given us new life in Jesus,
your Son.
May the Holy Spirit fill us with the grace
to help us be living signs of forgiveness
and love.

ALL: Amen.

LEADER: Jesus said, "I leave you peace.
My peace I give you."
Let us share that gift of peace
with one another
as Jesus shared it with us.

ALL: *Share a sign of peace.*

LEADER: May God fill your heart with kindness
to forgive others as he forgives you.

ALL: Amen.

LEADER: May almighty God bless you,
the Father, and the Son,
and the Holy Spirit.

ALL: Amen.

LEADER: Go in peace.

ALL: Thanks be to God.

Scripture Plays

The Scripture plays provide the children the opportunity to use their imaginations and creativity to tell the Scripture stories. Children often read these stories from the Bible or hear them read. Their vivid imaginations can picture what the scene might have been like. Encourage the children to use their imaginations as you prepare to use or present these plays in your group. Here are some tips for using and presenting these plays.

1 Be flexible and creative.
You can make these plays as simple or as involved as you choose and adapt them in a variety of ways to meet your setting and the time you have. As you read these plays, think of ways you might use them with the children. Several children can be assigned the various speaking parts and dramatically read the play to the whole group. With little planning and preparation, you can add costumes and simple actions and have the readers perform the play. You might also have the children present the play for parents or for other groups of children.

2 Enhance the scripts.
Children love to use their imaginations. Encourage the children to tell a story in their own words and to add some of their own dialogue to the play.

3 Consider costumes.
Simple costumes can be used for these plays. Look around the house and you can find many things that can be used for costumes. Bathrobes and towels can easily be made into tunics. Old sheets and large pieces of material can be draped around children and fashioned into outfits and costumes. Large sheets of paper or paper bags can be decorated to make costumes that identify the characters. Having each child decorate a hat with the name of the character is another way to identify each person in the play.

4 Add props.
Props can be simple things such as a tablecloth or a basket that are easy to find. Look around your room or your house for items you can use as props. Children have great imaginations and enjoy playing make-believe. Sometimes have the children make-believe they are using props. You might also have the children work together to draw things that represent the props and use them to act out the plays.

5 Set the scene.
Most of the settings can be simply imagined. At the start of a performance have the children close their eyes and imagine the setting. As the children are imagining the setting you might suggest some of the details. You might also have the children draw a background scene for the play on a large piece of mural paper. Children love to draw with colored chalk, and if your room has a chalkboard they could draw a background scene on the board. Often one child holding up a simple sign can tell the setting of the play.

The Lost Sheep

Based on Luke 15:4–6

Speaking Characters	Narrator 1 Narrator 2 Shepherd Lost sheep
Nonspeaking Characters	The shepherd's family, friends, and neighbors Flock of sheep

Flock   *The other sheep are gathered together in one place. Some of the sheep are walking around. Some are lying down.*

Shepherd   *The shepherd is walking among the sheep, looking for something he has lost. He looks very worried and is very concerned.*

Narrator 1   One day a shepherd was watching his sheep. He began walking among his flock. Then the shepherd discovered that one of his sheep was missing. He counted the sheep to make sure. Yes, one of the sheep was missing. The shepherd left the other sheep and immediately went to search for the lost sheep.

The shepherd leaves the flock, holding his staff in one hand and his other hand above his eyes. The shepherd looks off into the distance, turning his head in various directions. He says to himself:

Shepherd   Where is my lost sheep? I wonder if he wandered off into the hills? I must find the missing sheep before it gets dark. It will soon be nighttime and it will get very cold. The wolves will come out and might attack him.

The lost sheep is off in the distance. The sheep is walking in all directions showing that it is very lost.

Narrator 2   Feeling very, very unsafe, the lost sheep tried to find its way back to the flock.

Lost Sheep   How will I ever get back to my shepherd? I miss my parents, my brothers and sisters, and all my friends.

The shepherd is still looking for his sheep. He is walking up and down a hillside.

Narrator 1   The shepherd crossed streams and climbed up and down the hillside. Finally, he heard the lost sheep calling out. There in front of him he saw the sheep. The sheep was caught in a bush, calling out for help.

Lost Sheep   Baaa! Baaa!

Shepherd   There's my sheep. He's tangled in that bush. But he's safe. I have found you! Come here! I am so happy!

Narrator 2   The shepherd helped the lost sheep get out of the bush. Together they return happily to the other sheep.

The shepherd and the sheep walked toward the other sheep and the shepherd's family, friends, and neighbors. With a loud happy voice, the shepherd shouted out:

Shepherd   I have found my lost sheep! He was lost. He is now found.

Family, friends, and neighbors   *Everyone cheers and runs out to meet the shepherd and the lost sheep.*

CHAPTER 2 The Great Commandment

Based on Matthew 22:34–40

Speaking Characters
Narrator 1
Narrator 2
Narrator 3
Narrator 4
Scribe (teacher of the law)
Jesus

Nonspeaking Characters
People in crowd
Pharisees

The Pharisees and other people are standing around Jesus, who is teaching. Most of the people are attentively listening to Jesus. The Pharisees and a few of the people are looking at each other. They look confused at what Jesus is saying. One of the Pharisees, a teacher of the law, is waving his hand trying to get Jesus' attention.

Narrator 1
One day Jesus was teaching the people who had gathered to listen to him. Several Pharisees had joined the people. One of the Pharisees, who taught people about the Law of God, asked Jesus a question. But it was a trick question. He wanted to show the people that the Pharisees knew more about God's Law than Jesus knew.

The people look surprised. They are surprised that the teacher of the law is calling Jesus "Teacher" and asking Jesus such an important question.

Scribe
Teacher, what is the most important commandment?

Narrator 2
The people became very quiet. They knew that some of their leaders were following Jesus around and trying to get him in trouble.

Narrator 3
Jesus knew what the teacher of the law was trying to do. The answer that Jesus gave the teacher of the law was an answer the teacher already knew. It was an answer that was written in the Scriptures.

Jesus
The answer to your question is found in the Scriptures. There are two parts to the answer to your question. The two parts make up one answer. This is the answer to your question: Love God with all your heart, and soul, and mind. This is the first and greatest commandment. The second commandment is like the first: Love others as much as you love yourself.

The people look at the teacher of the law. They are wondering what he will say to Jesus.

The teacher of the law stands silently. He has nothing to say and no more questions to ask.

Narrator 4
Jesus' answer reminded the teacher of the law about the most important thing about God's Law. All God's laws help us love God, love other people, and love ourselves.

The Pharisees and the teacher of the law slowly turn away from Jesus.

The people are surprised once again. They watch as the Pharisees and the teacher of the law leave.

© RCL • Resources for Christian Living®

The Good Samaritan

Based on Luke 10:29–37

Speaking Characters
Narrator 1
Narrator 2
Samaritan

Nonspeaking Characters
Injured man   Traveler 1
Robber 1   Traveler 2
Robber 2   Innkeeper

Narrator 1 A man was traveling from Jerusalem to Jericho. The road went through the mountains. It was a long winding road with plenty of places for robbers to hide. Suddenly, two robbers attacked the traveler.

The robbers pantomime robbing the traveler. Both robbers run out from behind a rock where they have been hiding. Robber 1 holds the traveler down on the road and takes a money sack, which is tied to a cord around the traveler's waist. Robber 2 goes through the man's belongings and fills a sack with several items. Then both robbers run off down the road.

Narrator 2 The robbers took everything the traveler had. Running away they left the injured man lying in a ditch on the side of the road.

Lying on the side of the road, the injured traveler is waving and crying out for help.

A traveler stops and looks at the injured man. He looks off in the distance at Jerusalem and then at the sky. He takes one more look at the injured man and continues on his journey.

Narrator 1 A traveler came walking down the road. He was in a hurry to get where he was going. Deciding he had no time to stop, he continued on his journey.

As this traveler comes near the injured man, he crosses to the other side of the road. He acts as if he thinks that the injured man is a danger to him.

Narrator 2 Another traveler soon came down the road. He, too, stopped and looked at the injured man. He crossed to the other side of the road and quickly walked past the man.

The Samaritan is walking along the road with his donkey. He sees the man lying in the ditch and runs over to help.

Narrator 1 A man from the land of Samaria saw the injured man lying in the ditch and ran to help him.

Samaritan What has happened to you? Let me help you.

The Samaritan takes bandages and an oil jug from one of the bundles on the donkey. He cleans the injured man's wounds and bandages them. Finally he helps the injured man get on his donkey. Together they continue the journey until they come to an inn. The Samaritan knocks on the door of the inn, and an innkeeper answers.

Samaritan Take care of this man until I come back. Do whatever you need to do to help him get better. When I come back, I will pay you whatever it costs.

The innkeeper takes the money and nods in agreement. He takes the injured man inside and the Samaritan continues on his journey.

Zacchaeus

Based on Luke 19:1–10

Speaking Characters
Narrator
Jesus
Zacchaeus

Nonspeaking Characters
Disciples of Jesus
Townspeople

The townspeople are looking down the road. There is great excitement. Something important is about to happen. Then Jesus and his disciples appear, walking along the road into the town.

Zacchaeus is among the people and cannot see down the road. He is jumping up and down to see. Then he leaves the crowd and runs over to a tree, which he climbs.

Narrator One day Jesus and his disciples visited the town of Jericho on their way to Jerusalem. Many people from the town came out to greet Jesus. A tax collector named Zacchaeus was one of the people. Zacchaeus was very wealthy. The people did not like Zacchaeus because they felt that he cheated them. Zacchaeus could not see Jesus.

Zacchaeus Let me through. I want to see Jesus. Please let me through.

Narrator Zacchaeus was a short man and he could not see over the heads of the people in the crowd. Zacchaeus had an idea. He saw a sycamore tree. So he ran ahead of the people and climbed the tree.

Zacchaeus I'm going to climb this tree. Then I will be able to see Jesus.

Jesus and his disciples approach the tree and stop. Looking up at Zacchaeus, Jesus begins to talk with him.

Jesus Zacchaeus, come down out of the tree. Show me the way to your home. My disciples and I will stay at your house while we are in Jericho.

Zacchaeus, looking very surprised that Jesus wants to stay at his house, quickly climbs down from the tree.

Narrator Zacchaeus quickly climbed down from the tree. He was both very happy and very surprised. Zacchaeus knew that the people of the town did not like him. When Zacchaeus collected their taxes, he sometimes took money unfairly from them.

Some of the townspeople look angry that Jesus would want to go to Zacchaeus' home. They believe that Zacchaeus cheated them over and over again. Their anger turns to surprise as Zacchaeus comes to one of them and gives the person a sack full of money. They see how sorry Zacchaeus is. Giving the sack of money to one of the people in the crowd, Zacchaeus says:

Zacchaeus I have been unfair to the people, Jesus. I will give back four times the amount of money I have taken from them. I will also give half of everything I have to the poor.

Jesus Today, Zacchaeus, you have been saved.

The Forgiving Father

Based on Luke 15:11–24

Speaking Characters
Narrator 1
Narrator 2
Younger son
Father

Nonspeaking Characters
Workers

Narrator 1
Jesus often told the people stories to help them understand God's love for them. One day Jesus told the people the story about a man and his two sons.

The father and his younger son are having a serious discussion. The father looks very worried.

Narrator 2
There was a wealthy farmer who had two sons. The younger son decided that he was old enough to leave home and live on his own. But the son knew that he would need money. So the younger son told his father about his plans and asked for his share of the family's money.

Younger son
I am old enough now and I want to leave home. I want to live on my own. But, Father, I need my share of our family's money to do so. Please give me the share of the family money you have put aside for me.

The son is walking alongside a donkey, waving back to his father. The father is waving back.

Narrator 1
A few days later, the younger son packed up all of his belongings, took his money, and left home to live on his own.

The younger son is sitting down, holding his head in his hands. He is very worried.

Narrator 2
The younger son went to a country far away from his home. He spent his money foolishly. Soon he had no money left and could not even buy food. So he got a job feeding pigs.

The younger son pantomimes feeding pigs. He is holding a sack of grain, pouring it into a trough. He puts the sack down and sits on top of it and begins thinking.

Younger son
My father's servants have a lot of food to eat. These pigs always have food to eat every day, too. Yet I have very little food to eat.

I'm sorry that I ever left home. I'm going to go back home and I will tell my father that I am sorry.

The son gets up and begins walking toward his father's home. As he comes close to the home, the son sees the father running out to meet him. When they meet, they hug each other. Both have smiles on their faces. They are very happy.

Narrator 1
The son started walking home. When he got close to home, the son saw his father running down the road toward him. He began to run to his father. When they met, they hugged each other.

Younger son
Father, I am sorry. I was wrong to leave home. I will work for you.

The father is very happy. He turns and calls out to his workers who are standing in the distance.

Father
Bring out my best robe for my son. Bring food too, and let's celebrate because my son has come home.

The Gift of Peace

Based on John 14:15–27 and 20:21

Speaking Characters
Narrator 1
Narrator 2
Jesus

Nonspeaking Characters
Mary
Disciples

Scene One:
The Night Before Jesus Died

Jesus and the disciples are sitting around a table. They are sharing a meal and talking to one another.

Narrator 1   On the night before he died, Jesus ate a special meal with his disciples. During this meal Jesus and his disciples talked about many things. Jesus especially talked about God's love for them and how they were to love one another.

Narrator 2   Jesus also talked with his disciples about what it means to be one of his disciples. He taught them that they were to keep the commandments and that they were to love one another as he had loved them. He also made a special promise to them.

Jesus   If you love me you will keep my commandments. I will not leave you alone. I will ask the Father to send you the Holy Spirit in my name. The Holy Spirit will always be with you. The Holy Spirit will help you remember everything I have taught you. He will help you live as my disciples.

Narrator 1   Jesus then told the disciples something that they did not want to hear. He told them that he would soon be leaving them.

Jesus   Soon I will return to my Father. You will not be alone—ever. The Holy Spirit will come to you. I give you my gift of peace. Do not be sad, and do not worry. Be happy with me! I am going to the Father.

The disciples look sadly at one another. Then they look at Jesus.

Scene Two:
Three days after Jesus died and was buried

It is three days after Jesus died on the cross and was buried in the tomb. The disciples are together in a room. Their faces show that they are both very surprised and very happy. The Risen Jesus is with them

Jesus   Peace be with you. I now send you as the Father sent me.

Opening Rituals from the Catechist Guide

Blessing with Water

We Belong to God

Opening Ritual

Gathering

Gather the children around the baptismal font for this prayer ritual. Play a recording of instrumental music or an appropriate hymn. Invite the children to settle themselves and to become aware of God's presence among them.

Alternative: *Gather the children in the prayer area. In the center of the area place a table and on the table place a large bowl of water.*

LEADER: Let us begin by praying the Sign of the Cross to remind us of our Baptism.

ALL: *Bless themselves, saying,*
In the name of the Father, and of the Son, and of the Holy Spirit. Amen.

LEADER: Loving God, our Creator,
you are with us as we gather in prayer.
Open our hearts to your word.
We ask this in the name of your Son,
    Jesus Christ.

ALL: Amen.

Scripture Reading

Read aloud or invite a volunteer to read aloud the Scripture story "God Loves Us" (Luke 15:4–6) from the Bible. An adapted version of the Scripture story is found on page 6 of the child's book.

LEADER: Let us make the sign of the cross on our forehead, lips, and over our heart and ask the Holy Spirit to help us listen to the word of God.

READER: A reading from the holy gospel according to Luke.

ALL: Reverently sign their forehead, lips, and over their heart with the sign of the cross and then say,
Glory to you, Lord.

READER: Read the story aloud to the group. Conclude the reading, saying,
The gospel of the Lord.

ALL: Praise to you, Lord Jesus Christ.

Ritual: Signing with Water

LEADER: *Play a recording of appropriate instrumental music or an appropriate hymn. Invite the children to come forward one at a time. Dip your hand in the water and mark the child's forehead with the sign of the cross. Address the child by name and say,*
(Name), you belong to Christ. In the name of the Father, and of the Son, and of the Holy Spirit.

CHILD: Amen.

Closing

LEADER: Loving God, Creator and Father,
you call us by name;
we belong to you.
We thank you for the gift of water
that reminds us that you share your life
    and love with us.
Help us to live as children of God.
We ask this through Jesus Christ our Lord.

ALL: Amen.

© RCL • Resources for Christian Living®

Opening Ritual

Reverence for the Word of God

Gathering Procession

Play a recording of instrumental music or an appropriate hymn. Reverently hold a Bible (or the Book of the Gospels if available) in your hands at about eye level. As you process around the room, invite the children to process silently behind you to the prayer area. Upon arrival at the prayer area, invite the children to settle themselves and to become aware of God's presence among them.

Alternative 1: Reverently place the Bible (or the Book of the Gospels) in the prayer area. Invite the children to come forward and gather around the Scriptures. After they have gathered, invite the children to settle themselves and to become aware of God's presence among them.

Alternative 2: Invite the children to process from your room to an area in the church or chapel. Reverently hold the Bible in your hands at eye level and lead the children in the procession into the church or chapel.

Gathering Prayer

LEADER: Let us begin by praying the Sign of the Cross to remind us of our Baptism.

ALL: In the name of the Father, and of the Son, and of the Holy Spirit. Amen.

LEADER: God, our loving Father,
we gather around your word to us,
    the Sacred Scriptures.
Prepare our minds and hearts
to listen to your word.
We ask this through Jesus Christ our Lord.

ALL: Amen.

Scripture Reading

Read aloud or invite a volunteer to read aloud the Scripture story "The Great Commandment" (Matthew 22:34–40) from the Bible. An adapted version of the Scripture story is found on page 14 of the child's book.

LEADER: Let us make the sign of the cross on our forehead, lips, and heart and ask the Holy Spirit to help us listen to the word of God.

READER: A reading from the holy gospel according to Matthew.

ALL: *Reverently sign their forehead, lips, and over their heart with the sign of the cross and then say,*
Glory to you, Lord.

READER: *Read the story aloud to the group. Conclude the reading, saying,*
The gospel of the Lord.

ALL: Praise to you, Lord Jesus Christ.

Ritual

Play the instrumental version or the vocal version of the music used for the gathering procession. Then invite the children to come forward one at a time to reverence the Bible (or the Book of the Gospels). For example, the children may touch the book, kiss the book, or genuflect before the book.

Closing

LEADER: God, our loving Father,
today we show our reverence
    for your word, the Sacred Scriptures.
Send us the Holy Spirit
to help us remember
and follow your word every day.
We ask this through Christ our Lord.

ALL: Amen.

Jesus, Light of the World

Opening Ritual

Gathering

Gather the children in the church around the Easter candle. Play a recording of instrumental music or an appropriate hymn. Invite the children to settle themselves and to become aware of God's presence among them.

Alternative: Gather the children around a large candle in the prayer area. Play a recording of instrumental music or an appropriate hymn. Invite the children to settle themselves and to become aware of God's presence among them.

LEADER: Let us begin by praying the Sign of the Cross to remind us of our Baptism.

ALL: In the name of the Father, and of the Son, and of the Holy Spirit. Amen.

LEADER: God of goodness and mercy,
you send us the gift of the Holy Spirit.
Open our minds and hearts to
the Holy Spirit,
who is our teacher and helper.
We ask this through Jesus Christ our Lord.

ALL: Amen.

Scripture Reading

Read aloud or invite a volunteer to read aloud the Scripture story "The Good Samaritan" (Luke 10:29–37) from the Bible. An adapted version is found on page 22 of the child's book.

LEADER: Let us make the sign of the cross on our forehead, lips, and over our heart and ask the Holy Spirit to help us listen to the word of God with reverence.

READER: A reading from the holy gospel according to Luke.

ALL: *Reverently make the sign of the cross on their forehead, lips, and over their heart and then say,*
Glory to you, Lord.

READER: *Read the Scripture story aloud to the group. Conclude the reading, saying,*
The gospel of the Lord.

ALL: Praise to you, Lord Jesus Christ.

Ritual Candle Lighting

LEADER: *Gather around the Easter candle. Light the candle, saying,*
Jesus is the Light of the World.

Tell the children that Jesus asked us to be lights in our world. Ask the children to name things that the Holy Spirit can help them do to be lights in the world. For example, "Be kind to others," "Listen attentively to my parents," and so on.

After each statement, have the children respond,
Jesus, Light of the World,
help us to be lights in the world.

Closing

LEADER: God of goodness and mercy,
thank you for the gift of the Holy Spirit.
Send us the Holy Spirit
to help us to live as lights in the world.
We ask this through Jesus Christ our Lord.

ALL: Amen.

Praying the Our Father

Gathering

Gather the children in the prayer area. Play a recording of instrumental music or an appropriate hymn. Invite the children to settle themselves and to become aware of God's presence among them. Remind the children that Baptism makes us adopted children of God. Then say:

LEADER: Let us begin as we were baptized.

ALL: *Making the sign of the cross, say,*
In the name of the Father,
and of the Son,
and of the Holy Spirit. Amen.

LEADER: Loving God,
you are our Father.
Help us to know and trust your love for us.
Open our hearts to the Holy Spirit.
We ask this through Jesus Christ our Lord.

ALL: Amen.

Scripture Reading

Read aloud or invite a volunteer to read aloud the Scripture story "Zacchaeus" (Luke 19:1–10) from the Bible. An adapted version of the Scripture story is found on page 30 of the child's book.

LEADER: Let us make the sign of the cross on our forehead, lips, and over our hearts and ask the Holy Spirit to help us listen to the word of God.

READER: A reading from the holy gospel according to Luke.

ALL: *Reverently make the sign of the cross on their forehead, lips, and over their heart and then say,*
Glory to you, Lord.

READER: *Read the story aloud to the group. Conclude the reading, saying,*
The gospel of the Lord.

ALL: Praise to you, Lord Jesus Christ.

Ritual Prayer

Invite the children to pray the Our Father. If you are comfortable, lead them in praying the Our Father by slightly extending your arms and holding the palms of your hands upward. Share that this is a sign that we are opening our hearts to God's mercy and love.

LEADER: As a sign of our unity and that we are all children of God, let us pray together the prayer that Jesus taught us.

ALL: Our Father, who art in heaven,
hallowed be thy name;
thy kingdom come;
thy will be done on earth
as it is in heaven.
Give us this day our daily bread;
and forgive us our trespasses
as we forgive those who trespass
against us;
and lead us not into temptation,
but deliver us from evil. Amen.

Closing Prayer

LEADER: God, our loving Father,
we gather today to remember your great love for us.
Send us the Holy Spirit.
Help us to both forgive and seek forgiveness
and to live as your children.
We ask this through Jesus Christ our Lord.

ALL: Amen.

Laying On of Hands

Gathering

Gather the children in the prayer area. Play a recording of instrumental music or an appropriate hymn. Invite the children to settle themselves and to become aware of God's presence among them. Remind the children that at Baptism they receive the gift of the Holy Spirit and the grace to live as children of God.

LEADER: *Invite the children to pray, saying,*
Let us begin as we were baptized.

ALL: *Making the sign of the cross, say,*
In the name of the Father, and of the Son, and of the Holy Spirit. Amen.

LEADER: God, forgiving Father,
Jesus showed us how much you love us.
Send us the Holy Spirit
to help us trust your forgiveness
    and grace.
Open our hearts to listen to your word.
We ask this through Jesus Christ our Lord.

ALL: Amen.

Scripture Reading

Read aloud or invite a volunteer to read aloud the Scripture story "The Forgiving Father" (Luke 15:11–32) from the Bible. An adapted version of the Scripture story is found on page 38 of the child's book.

LEADER: Let us make the sign of the cross
on our forehead, lips, and over our heart
and ask the Holy Spirit to help us listen
to the word of God.

READER: A reading from the holy gospel
according to Luke.

ALL: *Reverently make the sign of the cross on their forehead, lips, and over their heart and then say,*
Glory to you, Lord.

READER: *Read the story aloud to the group. Conclude the reading, saying,*
The gospel of the Lord.

ALL: Praise to you, Lord Jesus Christ.

Ritual Laying On of Hands

LEADER: *Invite the children to come forward one at a time. Place your open hands on the head of each child, silently pray, and conclude by saying aloud,*
Remember that God always loves you.

CHILD: Thanks be to God.

LEADER: *After you have completed this ritual, say aloud,*
Let us now pray the prayer Jesus taught us.

ALL: Our Father . . .

Closing Prayer

LEADER: *Hold your hands outward, palms down, extended over the children, and pray,*
God, our forgiving Father,
you always love us.
Send the Holy Spirit of forgiveness
    upon these children.
Help them to trust in your forgiving love.
Help them to share your forgiving love
    with others.
We ask this in the name of Jesus Christ
    our Lord.

ALL: Amen.

© RCL • Resources for Christian Living®

Sharing a Sign of Peace

Gathering

Gather the children in the prayer area. Play a recording of instrumental music or an appropriate hymn. Invite the children to settle themselves and to become aware of God's presence among them. Remind the children that Baptism makes us followers of Jesus, who taught that children of God are peacemakers. Then say:

LEADER: Let us begin as we were baptized.

ALL: *Making the sign of the cross, say,*
In the name of the Father,
and of the Son,
and of the Holy Spirit. Amen.

LEADER: God, our loving Father,
you sent us your Son, the Prince of Peace.
Help us know and share the peace
that the Holy Spirit brings us.
Open our hearts to your word
that we may learn to live as peacemakers.
We ask this through Jesus Christ our Lord.

ALL: Amen.

Scripture Reading

Read aloud or invite a volunteer to read aloud the Scripture story "The Gift of Peace" (John 14:15–27 and 20:21) from the Bible. An adapted version of the Scripture story is found on page 46 of the child's book.

LEADER: Let us make the sign of the cross on our forehead, lips, and over our heart and ask the Holy Spirit to help us listen to the word of God.

READER: A reading from the holy gospel according to John.

ALL: *Reverently make the sign of the cross on their forehead, lips, and over their heart and then say,*
Glory to you, Lord.

READER: *Read the Scripture story (John 14:15–27 and 20:21) aloud to the group. Conclude the reading, saying,*
The gospel of the Lord.

ALL: Praise to you, Lord Jesus Christ.

Ritual Peace Greeting

LEADER: We are all children of God.
Let us pray as Jesus taught us:

ALL: Our Father, who art in heaven,
hallowed be thy name;
thy kingdom come;
thy will be done on earth
as it is in heaven.
Give us this day our daily bread;
and forgive us our trespasses
as we forgive those who trespass
against us;
and lead us not into temptation,
but deliver us from evil. Amen.

LEADER: Jesus gave the gift of his peace to his followers. Let us share that gift of peace with one another as Jesus did.

ALL: *Share a sign of peace.*

Closing

LEADER: God, our Father and giver of peace,
you sent us Jesus, your Son,
to show us how to live in peace
with you and with one another.
Send the Holy Spirit
to help us live as peacemakers.
We ask this through Jesus Christ our Lord.

ALL: Amen.

LEADER: The Lord frees us from our sins.
Live in peace.

ALL: Thanks be to God.

Part Six

Preparing
Older Children

About This Section

PART SIX • Preparing Older Children

The child's book for sacrament preparation that accompanies this series was written for ages seven to nine. This section is designed to include children ages ten to fifteen who are preparing for the sacrament of Reconciliation.

The handouts for older children, guide notes for catechists, and the guide notes for parents in this part of the manual include the same content and process as the child's book, the catechist guide, and the family guide. These materials have been adapted to be age-appropriate.

Since there may only be a few young people of these ages in your program, you may want to cluster the age groups or provide a small group of fully initiated young people to join in the preparation period as peer mentors.

This section includes:

- **Handouts for Older Children**
  —Copy these handouts as needed. You may want to put them in a small binder or folder for each participant.

- **Guide Notes for Catechists**
  —Copy these notes for each catechist who will be working with the older groups of children.

  —Refer to part five of this manual to make sure catechists have the materials they need.

- **Guide Notes for Parents**
  —Copy these notes for parents/families of the older children preparing for the sacrament.

  —Copy the opening ritual for each chapter, found in part five of this manual, and distribute them to the parents/families.

  —These notes were designed to assist families who are also preparing their older children at home for the sacrament.

CHAPTER 1 We Belong to God

FAITH FOCUS

What does it mean to belong to God?

Opening Ritual

In the opening prayer you were called by name and blessed with water. What was this experience like for you?

God Loves Us (Scripture)

Bible Background

In Jesus' time, the flocks of sheep could contain thousands of sheep. A flock would be made up of sheep and goats. During much of the year the flocks were out in the open. The shepherd endured great heat by day and chill and even frost by night. Sometimes the shepherd had to fight off wild beasts—hyenas, wolves, bears, and jackals all roamed the country-side—to protect the sheep. When a sheep wandered off and the shepherd's dog could not find it, the shepherd had to go out into deep valleys and climb cliffs to find it.

> **Think About It**
> *What descriptive words would you use to describe the relationship between a shepherd and his flock?*

Reading the Word of God

The writers of the Bible often describe God as the shepherd of his people. Look up and read this parable that Jesus told about a shepherd and his sheep. Discover what Jesus tells us about God in Luke 15:1–7.

> **Think About It**
> *What does this parable tell us about God's love for us?*

Understanding the Word of God

Jesus taught over and over again that we belong to God. To help us understand this important truth about God, Jesus told us that God is like a shepherd.

Because the people of Jesus' time knew all about shepherds and shepherding, they understood more clearly what Jesus was teaching.

The people knew that:
- the sheep and the shepherd truly felt that they belonged to one another.
- hearing the shepherd's voice, the sheep would follow him with trust.
- the shepherd would take great risks to protect the sheep from danger, search out the sheep when they wandered off, and lead the sheep to green pastures and water when food and water got scarce.

Knowing these things about the shepherd, Jesus' listeners would more easily understand what Jesus was telling them about God.

- We belong to God.
- We can always place our trust in God.
- God cares for us.
- God's love for us knows no limits.

> **Think About It**
> *What does it mean to call God our shepherd?*

Jesus, the Good Shepherd
(Doctrine/Liturgy)

The Bible story about the shepherd and the lost sheep tells us how much God loves us. Jesus, the Son of God, told another story about a shepherd.

The Good Shepherd

Jesus told this second story about sheep and a shepherd to describe his own love for his followers. Take the time to look up and read this story. You will find the story in John 10:1–18.

Jesus the Good Shepherd gave his life for us. He died on the cross and was raised from the dead to save us from our sins. Jesus' death and resurrection show us how much he loves us. Jesus is the Son of God. In telling this story, Jesus was telling his disciples how great God's love for people is.

Marked with the Sign of the Good Shepherd

We are joined to Jesus, the Good Shepherd, at Baptism. At the beginning of the celebration of Baptism, the priest or deacon calls us by name and says,

(Name), the Christian community welcomes you with great joy. In its name I claim you for Christ our Savior by the sign of the cross.

He traces a cross on our forehead. Then he invites our parents and godparents to do the same.

> **Think About It**
> *How does thinking about the story that Jesus told about the good shepherd help you understand the ritual of being signed with the cross at Baptism?*

Our Baptism

The Church celebrates Baptism because Jesus told his followers to baptize people. Baptism joins us to Jesus. We share new life in Christ. We share in Jesus' death and resurrection.

God shares his life with us. We become adopted children of God, our Shepherd, and members of our church family. Original sin and all other sins are forgiven. We receive the gift of the Holy Spirit. We are given the promise of eternal life.

> **Think About It**
> *What happens at Baptism?*

At Baptism we are marked with the sign of the cross. We are marked forever as followers of Jesus, the Good Shepherd. We belong to God forever.

> **Think About It**
> *What does it mean to call Jesus our shepherd?*

What do we celebrate at Baptism?

WHAT WE SEE AND HEAR

During the celebration of the sacrament of Reconciliation, the priest asks God's blessing on us. He does this by making the sign of the cross and praying, "In the name of the Father, and of the Son, and of the Holy Spirit." This reminds us that there are three Persons in one God— God the Father, God the Son, and God the Holy Spirit.

What Difference Does This Make in My Life?

Jesus taught that God is our shepherd. We belong to God. God knows and loves each of us by name. At Baptism God shares his life and love with us. We become adopted children of God. The Holy Spirit helps us share God's love with others.

MY FAITH DECISION

Talk with someone about one thing you will do this week to show God's love for people.

Read the words in the border that describe a good shepherd. Choose one of these qualities. Draw or write about how you might use that quality to be a good shepherd, or leader, who shows God's love for people.

Loyal Courageous Selfless Loyal Trustworthy
Selfless   Caring
Courageous   Faithful
Faithful Caring Trustworthy

TOGETHER AS A FAMILY

Remembering Together

In this chapter you learned that we belong to God in a special way. God knows and loves each of us. We become adopted children of God at Baptism. This is a good time for your family to talk about Baptism. Include responses to these or similar questions in the discussion:

- Where were you or your child baptized?
- Who baptized you?
- Who are your godparents?
- Who else was at your baptisms?
- Why were these special days?

Sharing Together

Choose one of the following activities to do together or design a similar activity of your own:

- Look at pictures in your family's photo albums that show each family member's baptism. Share stories about each baptism. Share why the name you gave your son or daughter is special and a sign of your love.
- In the Bible story the shepherd looked for the one lost sheep. Think of someone who may be lonely. Name something your family can do for that person.

 Visit the RCL sacraments web site by following the link titled "Sacraments" at www.FaithFirst.com.

Praying Together

Pray this or a similar prayer at family meals or at other family prayer times this week:

God, our Father,
we thank you for loving us
    and claiming us as your own.
Send the Holy Spirit
to help us live as your children.
We ask this through Jesus Christ
    our Lord. Amen.

Getting Ready Together

We begin the celebration of the sacrament of Reconciliation by praying the Sign of the Cross. This is a good time to review the meaning of the Sign of the Cross. The cross is a sign of God's mercy and love for us. At Baptism we are marked with the sign of the cross and claimed for Christ. When we pray the Sign of the Cross and bless ourselves, praying, "In the name of the Father, and of the Son, and of the Holy Spirit. Amen," we remember our baptism. We remember that we belong to Christ and are children of God.

CHAPTER 2 We Follow Jesus

FAITH FOCUS

What does the Great Commandment teach?

Opening Ritual

In the opening prayer we carried the Bible in procession. We gathered together and showed reverence for God's word. What was it like for you to show reverence for the word of God?

The Great Commandment
(Scripture)

Bible Background

The Old Testament tells the exciting story of how God entered into a covenant with the Israelites, the people God chose to be his people. God promised the Israelites that he would always be with them. They, in turn, promised to live as his people by obeying his laws, or commandments.

The Israelites called the first five books of their Scriptures the Torah. The Torah, which is also called the Pentateuch, contains the laws that guide God's people in living the covenant that God made with them and they made with God.

> *Think About It*
> What is the Torah?

Reading the Word of God

Look up and read Matthew 22:34–40. Discover what Jesus said about the laws, or commandments, that God had given to the Israelites.

> *Think About It*
> How did Jesus summarize the law that God had given to his people?

Understanding the Word of God

Jesus taught that he did not come to do away with the Law and the Prophets. He said that he came to fulfill them. Jesus revealed, or made known, the true meaning of the commandments and the message of the prophets.

Jesus taught that all God's commandments guide us in loving God, others, and ourselves. When the lawyer asked Jesus which commandment was the greatest, Jesus replied by giving him an answer the lawyer should have known. Jesus quoted two passages from the Torah.

Jesus quoted Deuteronomy 6:5 and Leviticus 19:18. Look up and read the two passages.

> *Think About It*
> What does the Great Commandment teach about showing reverence?

Jesus taught the Great Commandments both by his words and by his actions. His whole life teaches us how to show our love for God, for other people, and for ourselves.

Living a Holy Life (Doctrine/Liturgy)

The Great Commandment tells us that we are to love and respect God, ourselves, and all people.

Holiness

God created people in his own image and likeness. He created us to know him, love him, and serve him, and to live with him forever in eternal happiness. This is our life's job description. We are to live a life of holiness. We are to strive to love God with our whole mind, heart, soul, and strength. We do this when we live the Great Commandment.

One way we live the Great Commandment is to live the Ten Commandments. The first three commandments help us love and respect God. The last seven commandments help us love and respect ourselves and others. Through the commandments we have a surefire guide for living a life of holiness.

Conscience—God gives every person the gift of a conscience to help us know the commandments. Our conscience helps us know what is right and what is wrong. It helps us know what God wants us to do and not to do.

Free will—God also gives every person the gift of a free will. This means that we can choose to live or not to live the commandments. When we live God's command-ments, we live a holy life. We show that we belong to God. We are children of God.

Think About It
What job description has God given us? How do the commandments, conscience, and free will work together to help us live that job description?

The Sacrament of Penance

Jesus gave us the sacraments. The sacraments celebrated in the liturgy are signs given to us by Christ. But they are more than signs. The sacraments make us sharers in God's own life. Christ touches our lives and we are changed. We receive the grace to grow as children of God and to live a holy life.

Penance is one of the sacraments. This sacrament is also called by other names. It is called the sacrament of Reconciliation. We can celebrate this sacrament together with other members of our church family and the priest. Or we can celebrate it individually with the priest.

We celebrate this sacrament for the first time before we receive First Communion. In the sacrament of Reconciliation we are forgiven the sins that we commit after we are baptized. We sin when we freely choose to do what we know is against what God wants us to do. We also sin when we choose not to do something we know God wants us to do. Every sin hurts our friendship with God and with other people.

Think About It
Why do we celebrate the sacraments? Why do we celebrate Penance?

FAITH FOCUS

What is the sacrament of Reconciliation?

WHAT WE SEE AND HEAR

The crucifix reminds us that Jesus' dying on the cross shows his love for his Father and for us. We see the crucifix in our church. We also see the crucifix in the reconcilia-tion room. The crucifix reminds us of the way that Jesus lived the Great Commandment.

What Difference Does This Make in My Life?

Jesus gave us the sacrament of Reconciliation. When we celebrate this sacrament, our sins are forgiven and we receive the grace to live the Great Commandment. The Holy Spirit teaches us and helps us live holy lives.

MY FAITH DECISION

Talk with someone about one thing that you will do this week to live the Great Commandment.

Name someone who is living the Great Commandment.

_____

_____

Describe what the person is doing that makes a difference.

_____

_____

Describe how you can live the Great Commandment.

_____

_____

Describe how that will help you make a difference.

_____

_____

TOGETHER AS A FAMILY

Remembering Together

In this chapter you learned about the Great Commandment. The Great Commandment teaches that we are to live a holy life. We are to love God with our whole heart and soul, and we are to love others as we love ourselves (see Matthew 22:34–40). Talk about living the Great Commandment. Use these or similar questions:

- How does our family help one another live the Great Commandment?
- Who are models for living the Great Commandment?
- How does our conscience help us to live the Great Commandment?
- How do we show we are sorry when we do not live the Great Commandment?

Sharing Together

Choose one of these activities to do together or design a similar activity of your own:

- Watch a favorite TV show together. Afterward discuss how the people in the show are living or not living the Great Commandment.

- Have each family member write on an index card how your family can live the Great Commandment. Choose one thing that you will do together.
- Talk about ways your family can resolve to settle conflicts peacefully.

 Visit the RCL sacraments web site by following the link titled "Sacraments" at www.FaithFirst.com.

Praying Together

Pray this or a similar prayer at family meals or at other family prayer times this week:

God, our loving Father,
you gave us the Great Commandment.
Send us the Holy Spirit
to help us live the Great Commandment
   every day.
We ask this through Jesus Christ
   our Lord. Amen.

Getting Ready Together

This is an appropriate time to briefly review the parts of the rites of Reconciliation together. Go through the rite of Reconciliation that will be celebrated, "The Individual Rite for Reconciliation" or "The Communal Rite for Reconciliation."

CHAPTER 3 We Listen to the Holy Spirit

What does the parable of the Good Samaritan teach us?

Opening Ritual

In the opening prayer we lit a candle. We talked about how the Holy Spirit is always with us.

What was it like for you to pray around the lighted candle?

The Good Samaritan (Scripture)

Bible Background

People of Jesus' time honored Jesus with the title Rabbi, or Teacher. Like other teachers Jesus often used a story to get his point across to his listeners. One type of story Jesus used is called a parable. Parables often have a surprise ending. The surprise helps the people hearing the parable understand the message of the teacher.

> ***Think About It***
> *What parables can you name that Jesus told?*

Reading the Word of God

Look up and read the parable in Luke 10:29–37. A Samaritan is the main character of the parable. Jesus' listeners did not think that Samaritans were faithful children of God. Discover the surprise ending of the parable.

> ***Think About It***
> *What did the Samaritan choose to do? Why do you think the ending of the story may have surprised Jesus' listeners?*

Understanding the Word of God

A parable compares one thing to another to help listeners or readers understand the main point of the story.

In the parable of the Good Samaritan Jesus compares two leaders of the people of God, a priest and a Levite, with the Samaritan. By doing this Jesus makes the point that all people are called to be good neighbors. All people receive grace to live the Great Commandment.

Jesus is also teaching that it is not enough to only say that we believe in God. We must also live as children of God. Jesus is teaching his followers that it is not enough to be baptized and call oneself a follower of Jesus. We must live our faith in Jesus. We must live as Jesus taught and showed us how to live. We must live as followers of Jesus.

> ***Think About It***
> *How was the Samaritan a light in the world? How are you a light in the world?*

At Baptism we are given a candle, which has been lighted from the Easter candle. As we receive this candle we are told, "Receive the light of Christ. . . . [W]alk always as children of the light" (*Rite of Baptism* 64). The way we live is to be a sign that we are followers of Jesus, the Light of the World.

We Make Good Decisions
(Doctrine/Liturgy)

The Samaritan made a good decision. He chose to stop and help the injured traveler.

Making Good Decisions

Followers of Christ need to make good decisions and put our decisions into action as the Samaritan did. When we put our good decisions into action, we show we are followers of Jesus, the Light of the World.

Here are some of the things you can do to learn to make good decisions.

- Pray to the Holy Spirit.
- Read, study, and pray over the word of God.
- Learn what Jesus taught about the Great Commandment, the Ten Commandments, and the Beatitudes.
- Learn what our church family teaches about how we are to live as children of God.
- Talk over our decisions— before and after we make them—with parents, teachers, and other adults.
- Ask the help of parents, teachers, and other adults.
- Choose what we know is the right thing to do and do it.

Think About It
How do you go about making a good decision? What might you do better?

Sin: A Bad Decision

We do not always make good decisions. We sometimes choose to sin. We deliberately turn our hearts away from God. To help us understand more clearly what sin is all about, the Church speaks about sin in many ways. Here are two ways:

Mortal sin—Mortal sin breaks our relationship with God. It is a serious failure in one's love for God, for oneself, and for other people.

Venial sin—Venial sin weakens but does not break our relationship with God.

It is important that we accept responsibility for all of our decisions, including our sins.

Think About It
Why is sin a bad decision?

Sacrament of Confession

In Reconciliation we confess, or tell, our sins to the priest. This is why it is sometimes called the sacrament of confession. We must confess any mortal sin we commit. We may also confess venial sins. Because all sin turns our heart away from God's love, we should seek forgiveness of all sins, including venial sins.

Sacrament of Conversion

When we celebrate the sacrament of Reconciliation, we show that living as a child of God is important to us. This shows we want to do our best to live as Jesus taught us. This is why it is sometimes called the sacrament of conversion.

Think About It
How does the sacrament of Reconciliation help us to live as lights in the world?

Whenever we think about our sins, we must remember that God wants to forgive us.

FAITH FOCUS

What does it mean to confess our sins in the sacrament of Reconciliation?

WHAT WE SEE AND HEAR

We can confess our sins to the priest either face-to-face or kneeling behind a screen. The priest will never tell anyone what we confess to him.

What Difference Does This Make in My Life?

The sacrament of Reconciliation brings God's love and forgiveness into our lives right now. The Holy Spirit helps us make decisions to show our love for God and for others.

You see an advertisement calling for an outline for a new television series. The series is about a group of young people who make a decision to live as followers of Christ in the world. Write your outline here.

MY FAITH DECISION

Talk with someone about one thing you will do this week to help you live as a light in the world.

TOGETHER AS A FAMILY

Remembering Together

In this chapter you learned that followers of Jesus are good Samaritans. As followers of Jesus, we are to strive to make good decisions that bring light to the world. Discuss responses to these or similar questions:

- How does our family help one another make good choices?
- How is our family a light in the world?
- How do we celebrate being lights in the world?

Sharing Together

Choose one of these activities to do together or design a similar activity of your own:

- Light a candle during mealtime. Let the candle remind you that God has called you by name to be followers of Jesus, the Light of the World.
- Watch the television news together. Identify people who were good Samaritans. Choose one thing that your family members can do to be good Samaritans.
- Write a prayer to the Holy Spirit, asking for help to make good decisions. Pray the prayer as a family this week.

 Visit the RCL sacraments web site by following the link titled "Sacraments" at www.FaithFirst.com.

Praying Together

Pray this or a similar prayer at family meals or at other family prayer times this week:

> God, our loving Father,
> today we gather to listen to
>   the Holy Spirit.
> We know that the Holy Spirit is
>   always with us
> to help us choose light over darkness.
> May the Holy Spirit help us live
>   as lights in the world.
> We ask this through Jesus Christ
>   our Lord Amen.

Getting Ready Together

Go through the "Confession of Sins" part of the rite of Reconciliation together. Emphasize that confessing our sins in this sacrament is one way we show that we take responsibility for our sins. Reassure your son or daughter that the priest will not tell anyone what he or she confesses in the sacrament of Reconciliation.

CHAPTER 4

We Are Sorry

FAITH FOCUS

What does the gospel story about Zacchaeus teach us about being sorry?

Opening Ritual

In the opening prayer we prayed together. What was it like for you to pray the Our Father with our group?

Zacchaeus (Scripture)

Bible Background

In Jesus' time, the Romans occupied and governed Palestine, the homeland of Jesus. The Romans taxed the people to finance their governing of Palestine. Normally, the task of collecting the taxes was given to a local resident. The Romans would set the amount to be collected from a village. The tax collector would then owe only that amount to the Roman authorities. Anything over and above that amount the tax collector would keep as his profit. This way of collecting taxes would often result in the people paying more taxes than the Romans required.

Think About It
Why do you think the people of Jesus' time hated tax collectors?

Reading the Word of God

Look up and read the gospel story in Luke 19:1–10, "Zacchaeus the Tax Collector." Discover what Zacchaeus did to show that he was truly sorry for treating the people of Jericho unfairly.

Think About It
What did Zacchaeus do to make up with the people of Jericho?

Understanding the Word of God

In this gospel story Jesus invites himself to be a guest in Zacchaeus' home. The people are completely surprised—and even angry—that Jesus would invite himself to stay at the home of such a terrible sinner as a tax collector. Jesus adds to their surprise by telling Zacchaeus that salvation has come to him.

Divine mercy—The name *Jesus* means "God who saves." This gospel story passes on the faith of the Church that all Jesus' words and actions reveal that God extends his mercy and forgiveness to all people. God loves all people, even people despised and hated by others as Zacchaeus was.

True sorrow—Zacchaeus responded to Jesus by saying that he would repay everyone from whom he had unfairly taken more taxes than they owed. This action of Zacchaeus reveals what it means to be truly sorry for our sins. True sorrow includes making up for or repairing the harm caused by our sins.

Think About It
Why is repairing the harm caused by sin a necessary part of true sorrow for sin?

God desires that all people, without exception, share in his love and life both on earth and forever in heaven.

We Tell God We Are Sorry
(Doctrine/Liturgy)

Zacchaeus showed he was sorry for his sins. We too need to show we are sorry for our sins. Being sorry is a sign of love. It shows our love for God and for other people.

The Spirit of Forgiveness

The Holy Spirit helps us to be truly sorry for our sins. The Holy Spirit invites us to turn to God and to other people and say,

"I am sorry. I ask for your forgiveness."

The Holy Spirit also guides and teaches us to forgive others. When someone shows us they are sorry and says, "I am sorry. I ask for your forgiveness," the Holy Spirit opens our heart to forgive them.

When we forgive others, we treat them the way God treats us. We are living the Beatitude "Blessed are people who show mercy to others" (based on Matthew 5:7). People who are merciful are living as children of God. God promises that they will receive his mercy.

Contrition

Contrition, or true sorrow for sins, is a necessary part of the sacrament of Reconciliation. In the celebration of this sacrament, we show God we are sorry for our sins.

Penance—After we confess our sins to the priest, he gives us a penance. A penance is a prayer that we say or an action that we do to show we are truly sorry. Our penance helps us to repair, or heal, the harm we have caused by our sins.

Act of contrition—After we accept our penance, we pray an act of contrition, or a prayer of sorrow. When we pray this prayer,

- we tell God we are sorry for our sins with all our heart.
- we promise to do our penance and not to sin again.
- we promise to heal the harm we have caused by our sins.
- we ask God to help us avoid temptation. Temptation is whatever leads us to sin.
- we ask God's mercy in the name of Jesus.

Think About It
How can we show that we are truly sorry for our sins?

When we are sorry for our sins and strive to make amends for our sins, we are showing that we are responding to the Holy Spirit. We share in God's love and mercy. We are made one again with God and with one another.

FAITH FOCUS

In Reconciliation how do we show we are truly sorry for our sins?

WHAT WE SEE AND HEAR

The priest usually wears a purple stole for the celebration of the sacrament of Reconciliation. The color purple is a sign of penance. The stole looks like a long scarf. It is worn by priests and bishops around their neck and over both shoulders.

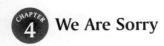
What Difference Does This Make in My Life?

In Reconciliation we show God we are sorry and ask for forgiveness. The Holy Spirit helps us to be sorry for our sins and to make up for our sins. We receive the grace to forgive others as God forgives us.

Making up is sometimes easy, sometimes difficult. Making up is sometimes embarrassing. It is not always easy to say "I'm sorry." It is not always easy to say "I forgive you." How long would a friendship last if we wouldn't or just plain couldn't make up?

Write a prayer to the Holy Spirit. Ask the Holy Spirit to give you a merciful heart— a heart capable of true sorrow and of forgiving all who wrongfully offend you.

MY FAITH DECISION

Talk with someone about one thing that you can do or say this week to show you are sorry.

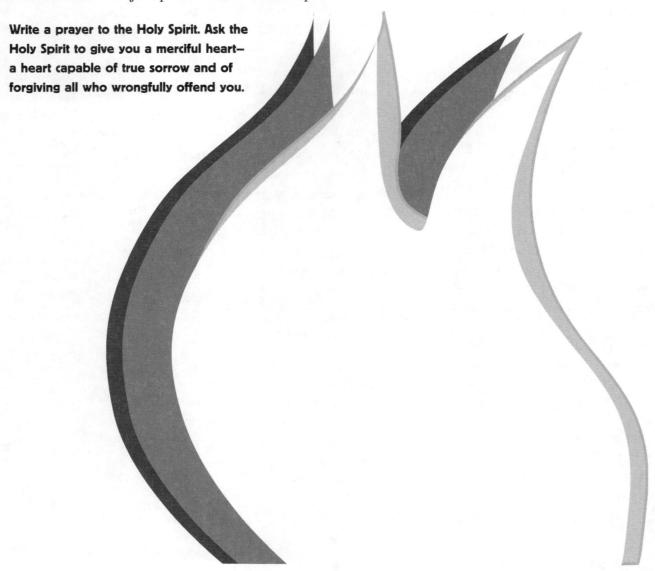

TOGETHER AS A FAMILY

Remembering Together

In this chapter you learned about Zacchaeus and what it means to be truly sorry for one's sins. Talk about what you learned in this chapter. Share responses to these or similar questions:

- What did Jesus teach about being sorry for our sins?
- What did Zacchaeus show us about being truly sorry for the harm we wrongfully cause other people?
- How do our family members show each other that we are truly sorry?
- How does our family share forgiveness with each other?
- How do we show that we have made up, or reconciled, with each other?

Sharing Together

Choose one of these activities to do together or design a similar activity of your own:

- Retell a family story about forgiveness.
- Talk about the importance of family members being truly sorry and asking for and giving forgiveness when they wrongfully offend each other.
- Share ideas about ways your family can be forgiving. Choose one thing that you will do together.
- Make a centerpiece for the table. Write the words "Forgive and Seek Forgiveness" on the bottom half of an index card. Fold the index card in half and stand the centerpiece on your table to serve as a reminder for your family to be a forgiving people.

 Visit the RCL sacraments web site by following the link titled "Sacraments" at www.FaithFirst.com.

Praying Together

Pray this or a similar prayer at family meals or at other family prayer times this week:

God, our loving Father,
today we gather to remember
your great love.
Send us the Holy Spirit
to help us both forgive and
seek forgiveness.
We ask this through Jesus Christ
our Lord. Amen.

Getting Ready Together

Continue to review the parts of the rites of Reconciliation together. Take time to share ideas about the importance of accepting and doing the penance we receive in this sacrament. Read the words of an act of contrition together. Talk about the meaning of the prayer.

We Are Forgiven

FAITH FOCUS

What does the gospel story about the forgiving father teach us about God's love for us?

Opening Ritual

In the opening prayer we placed our hands on each other's heads.

What was it like for you to celebrate that ritual?

The Forgiving Father (Scripture)

Bible Background

The Bible, from one important point of view, can be read as the story of forgiveness. It is the story of God's people turning their back on God's love, and God constantly reaching out and forgiving his people.

In the Scriptures that story is told both in narrative and in poetry by the prophets. The prophets were those chosen by God to speak in his name. They offer God's invitation to the people to return to God's love.

In the Old Testament the message of the prophets is found in the prophetic books. The greatest of all the prophets is Jesus Christ, the Word of God.

> *Think About It*
> *What did the prophets in the Old Testament do?*

Reading the Word of God

Look up and read Luke 15:11–32, the parable of the forgiving father. Discover how the father treated his son.

> *Think About It*
> *What did the father do to show that he welcomed his son back home? What did the son do to earn the father's forgiveness?*

Understanding the Word of God

In story after story Jesus assures people, especially people whom others judged to be sinners, that God loves them. God waits for them to return home—to turn to him in trust as the son in the gospel story turned to his father.

The writers of the Old Testament use the word *hesed* to describe this love of God. Understanding the meaning of this word helps us both to understand this gospel parable and to gain some understanding of how much God loves us.

There is no one English word or idea that captures the meaning of the Hebrew word *hesed*. All these ideas are contained in this Hebrew word:

● loyalty
● trustworthiness
● generosity and kindness without limits, or mercy
● justice
● peace
● salvation
● helping those who suffer and are helpless

> *Think About It*
> *In the parable of the forgiving father, which of the above qualities do you think belonged to the father? How do these qualities help you turn toward God when you sin?*

Jesus tells us that God is always waiting with outstretched arms to welcome us home. God welcomes everyone who sins to return to his love.

The Gift of Forgiveness
(Doctrine/Liturgy)

When we sin, God does not move away from us. We move away from, or even turn our back on, God's love.

Forgiveness

In the parable of the forgiving father Jesus tells us that God always forgives us when we are truly sorry for our sins. God will forgive any and all sins. More than that, this parable tells us that God rejoices when we turn to him for forgiveness.

Baptism—The sacraments make us sharers in God's mercy and forgiving love. In Baptism original sin and all personal sins, mortal and venial, we commit before Baptism are forgiven. Baptism is the first and chief sacrament for the forgiveness of sin. We are united to Christ, who died and was raised from the dead, and gave us the gift of the Holy Spirit.

> **Think About It**
> *Why do we call Baptism a sacrament of forgiveness?*

Eucharist—When we celebrate the Eucharist, we share in God's forgiving love. All venial sins are forgiven and we receive the grace to avoid sin. Through the Eucharist we grow closer to God and to one another.

> **Think About It**
> *How does the Eucharist reconcile us with God and with one another?*

Words of Forgiveness— The Prayer of Absolution

Sins committed after Baptism are normally forgiven in the sacrament of Reconciliation. Reconciliation is one of the Sacraments of Healing. In this sacrament the Holy Spirit reconciles us with God and with one another.

In the sacrament of Reconciliation Christ is present in the Church. Through the ministry of bishops and priests we are forgiven our sins. After we confess our sins, accept our penance, and tell God we are truly sorry, we receive absolution. *Absolution* means "pardon from sins."

The bishop or priest holds his hand over our head or places his hand on our head. He makes the sign of the cross over us as he says, in the name of Christ,
I absolve you from your sins in the name of the Father, and of the Son, and of the Holy Spirit.

We make the sign of the cross as the priest blesses us. Then we respond, "Amen."

In Reconciliation we are forgiven our sins. We are reconciled with God and with the Church. We look forward to living together with God, Jesus, Mary, and all the saints in heaven.

> **Think About It**
> *What does the prayer of absolution tell us about God's love?*

FAITH FOCUS

In Reconciliation what is the sign of God forgiving our sins?

WHAT WE SEE AND HEAR

In the sacrament of Reconciliation the priest extends his hands over our head as he prays the prayer of absolution. This gesture of laying on of hands is used in this sacrament as a sign that the Holy Spirit is at work.

What Difference Does This Make in My Life?

Forgiveness is a sign of love. It is a sign of God's love for us and of our love for other people. In the sacrament of Reconciliation we share in God's forgiving love. We are forgiven the sins we commit after Baptism. We receive the grace to forgive others.

MY FAITH DECISION

Talk with someone about one thing you will do this week to be forgiving.

Think of a time when a friend said or did something that hurt your feelings, but that person did not seem to be aware that your feelings were hurt. How would you respond to that person? How can you be a sign of God's forgiving love to that person? List words or phrases that describe what you might say or do to reconcile with your friend.

TOGETHER AS A FAMILY

Remembering Together

In this chapter you listened to the parable of the forgiving father. In the sacrament of Reconciliation God forgives us our sins. God shows us that he always loves us. Discuss responses to these or similar questions:

- How does our family help each other to be forgiving?
- How does our family show that we forgive each other?
- How does forgiveness help our family share our love with each other?

Sharing Together

Sharing forgiveness shows our love for one another. Choose one of these activities to do together or design a similar activity of your own:

- Take turns sharing stories about times when you forgave each other. Talk about how these experiences were a sign of your love for one another.
- Write a prayer together to the Holy Spirit asking for help to be forgiving. Pray the prayer together this week.

- Share ideas about ways each member of your family can be like the forgiving father to each other. Choose one thing that you will do together.

 Visit the RCL sacraments web site by following the link titled "Sacraments" at www.FaithFirst.com.

Praying Together

Pray this or a similar prayer at family meals or at other prayer times this week:

God, our loving Father,
you send us the Holy Spirit.
Help us forgive one another
  as you forgive us.
We ask this through Jesus Christ
  our Lord. Amen.

Getting Ready Together

Continue to review the parts of the rite of Reconciliation together. In particular take time to read the words of the prayer of absolution together. Talk about the meaning of this prayer.

CHAPTER 6 We Are Peacemakers

FAITH FOCUS

What gift did Jesus give to his followers before he returned to his Father?

Opening Ritual

In the opening prayer we shared a sign of peace with one another.

What was it like for you to share a sign of peace?

The Gift of Peace (Scripture)

Bible Background

The English word *peace* translates the Hebrew word *shalom* and the Greek word *irene*. Like the Hebrew word *hesed,* which you learned about in chapter 5, there is no single English word that captures the meaning of either the Hebrew or Greek word for *peace.*

In the Old Testament the word *peace* points to our communion, our living in harmony, with God. In the New Testament, it points to our communion with God through Jesus Christ. This peace, communion with God, is the gift of Jesus to all people.

> **Think About It**
> What does the word peace *mean?*

Reading the Word of God

Look up and read John 14:15–27 and John 20:21. Discover Jesus' final gift to his disciples.

> **Think About It**
> How important do you think it was to the disciples to receive the gift of peace from Jesus?

Understanding the Word of God

Jesus shared the gift of God's peace with his disciples. Jesus told the disciples that when they entered a home they should say, "Peace be to all who live here." Paul the Apostle begins many of his letters by sharing a greeting of peace with his readers.

One title that Christians give to Jesus is the Prince of Peace. When we understand the true meaning of the word *peace,* as Jesus used it and the writers of the Bible used it, we can truly understand the meaning of this title. Jesus came to earth to bring us the gift of living in communion with God and with one another.

In Jesus and through Jesus our communion with God is restored. We are reconciled with God and with one another. We receive the grace of the Holy Spirit to live as children of God, harmoniously with God and with one another. That is the peace Jesus Christ gives. It is that peace that Christians are called to share with one another—and with all people.

> **Think About It**
> Why do you think that Jesus called peacemakers children of God? How can you share Christ's peace with others?

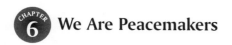

Blessed Are the Peacemakers
(Doctrine/Liturgy)

Jesus taught that we are to share the gift of peace with others. He said,

"Blessed are the peacemakers. They are children of God."

BASED ON MATTHEW 5:9

Peacemakers

Jesus told his disciples that they were to be peacemakers. As Jesus brought God's peace to all, his followers were to do the same.

Our Church teaches us that peacemakers act justly. This means that we love and treat people fairly. We are kind to people, even to people who are unkind to us. We respect all people. All people are children of God. God created people in his image and likeness.

We live as peacemakers when we keep the commandments and live as Jesus taught. We are peacemakers when we love others as Jesus loved us. We are peacemakers when we forgive others as God forgives us. We live as peacemakers when we ask others to forgive us.

As Jesus gave his disciples the gift of the Holy Spirit, we too have received the gift of the Holy Spirit. The Holy Spirit gives us the courage to live as peacemakers. This is not always easy to do.

> ***Think About It***
> *What are some of the qualities, or characteristics, of a Christian peacemaker?*

Sacrament of Peace

In the sacrament of Reconciliation, God forgives our sins. We are reconciled with God and with the Church. We are at peace with God and the Church.

At the end of the celebration of the sacrament, the priest tells us,

Go in peace,
and proclaim to the world
the wonderful works of God
who has brought you forgiveness.

We respond, "Amen."

We are reconciled with God and with one another. We are to go forth and share the gifts of forgiveness and peace with others.

We want everyone to know how wonderful God's love is. We want everyone to know how wonderful it is to live in peace with God and one another.

> ***Think About It***
> *At the end of the celebration of Reconciliation, why do you think the priest says, "Go in peace"?*

Through the grace of the Holy Spirit we are made living signs of the kingdom of peace, the kingdom of God. There we will live in eternal peace with God, Jesus, Mary, and the saints forever.

FAITH FOCUS

Why do we share the gift of peace with others?

WHAT WE SEE AND HEAR

Blessings are one of the ways the Church shows that God always shares his love with us. All our blessings remind us that God, who knows and loves each of us by name, is always with us. This is the greatest blessing we could have.

© RCL • Resources for Christian Living®

What Difference Does This Make in My Life?

We forgive others as God forgives us because we are children of God. We are kind to others as God is kind to us. We are merciful to others as God is merciful to us. We are peacemakers.

MY FAITH DECISION

Talk with someone about one thing that you will do this week to live as a peacemaker.

Blessed Are the Peacemakers

Jesus said, "Blessed are the peacemakers."
Who do you know who is a peacemaker? What does that person do?

_____ is a peacemaker because

_____

_____

_____ .

How can you be a peacemaker?

I can be a peacemaker by _____

_____

_____

_____

_____

_____ .

TOGETHER AS A FAMILY

Remembering Together

In this chapter you listened to the Bible story of Jesus giving the disciples the gift of peace. We receive the gift of God's peace and give thanks to God for that gift in the sacrament of Reconciliation. Discuss responses to these or similar questions:

- How does the Holy Spirit help our family live as peacemakers?
- How does our family share Jesus' gift of peace with each other?
- How does our family live as peacemakers in the world?

Sharing Together

Choose one of these activities to do together or design a similar activity of your own:

- Watch television together. When violence is portrayed, discuss the causes and effects of that violence. Talk about ways people can peacefully solve the conflicts shown.
- Make a symbol of the Holy Spirit, such as a flame. Display the symbol where it can remind everyone to live as peacemakers.

 Visit the RCL sacraments web site by following the link titled "Sacraments" at www.FaithFirst.com.

Praying Together

The Holy Spirit is our helper, teacher, and guide. Make this prayer to the Holy Spirit a prayer your family prays each day as you begin the final preparation for the celebration of the sacrament of Reconciliation.

Come, Holy Spirit, fill the hearts
   of your faithful.
And kindle in them the fire of your love.
Send forth your Spirit and they
   shall be created.
And you will renew the face of the earth.
Amen.

Getting Ready Together

Continue sharing the parts of the rite of Reconciliation together. In particular review the dismissal and thanksgiving rites. Talk about the meaning of the words. As you make final preparations for the celebration of the sacrament of Reconciliation, go through the entire rite of Reconciliation that will be celebrated. Begin and end with a short prayer, for example:

God and Father of us all,
you forgive our sins and send us
   the gift of your peace.
Help us forgive each other and
   work together for peace
   in the world.

BASED ON THE *RITE OF PENANCE* 211

We Belong to God

Background

The Lord Is My Shepherd

Images can help people express concepts in tangible, concrete ways. One of the central images the writers of the Sacred Scriptures used to describe God's love for his people was the image of God as the shepherd of his people. The power and depth of the meaning of this image of a shepherd can be lost to those living in a highly technological, contemporary environment. Perhaps the depth of its meaning can be more easily grasped by people today living in a rural environment and caring for land and livestock. The first hearers of the message of the Scriptures knew the special loving, caring, dedicated bond that united sheep and shepherd. The sheep knew the voice of the shepherd and responded to the shepherd's voice. It was only with great difficulty that a strange voice could lure a sheep away.

A good shepherd would go to great lengths to care for his sheep. For example, a good shepherd would sleep in front of the entrance way to the place the sheep were gathered so that beasts would have to climb over the shepherd's body to get to the sheep. Jesus, the Son of God, revealed that love. He chose death on the cross for his lost sheep. In Baptism we share in the death and resurrection of Jesus. Our sins are forgiven. We are reborn to new life in Jesus. We receive the promise of eternal life in heaven.

More background: For further reading and reflection see *Catechism of the Catholic Church* 218–221, 575, 582, 588, 754, 764, and 1465.

First Thoughts

Caring

When children experience the caring of someone who loves them, they come to know security and trust. When caring is absent from a relationship, they may experience abandonment and fear.

Cared-for children in turn enjoy and value caring for other people, animals, flowers, plants, toys—you name it. Engage children in caring projects and they seem to light up with joy and enthusiasm and a growing sense of responsibility. Make caring a cornerstone of your time with the children. As children sense being cared for and develop the virtue, or good habit, of caring for others, they get a glimpse of the unique relationship God has entered into with them.

Children of God

In his important document on catechesis *Catechesi Tradendae (On Catechesis in Our Time)*, Pope John Paul II wrote: "The definitive aim of catechesis is to put people not only in touch but in communion, in intimacy, with Jesus Christ" (5). Facilitating the children's growth in intimacy and communion with Jesus Christ is a major responsibility of catechists. Use the wonderful image of the shepherd to help the children grow in this intimacy and communion with God. Remind the children that God has called them his children. Invite them to call upon the Holy Spirit to help them lovingly call God "Abba" as Jesus did.

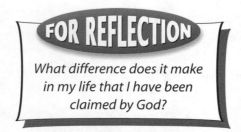

FOR REFLECTION

What difference does it make in my life that I have been claimed by God?

Overview

FAITH FOCUS

We share new life in Christ through Baptism. Through Baptism God shares with us divine life. Baptism marks us as belonging to Jesus the Good Shepherd.

OBJECTIVES

After completing this chapter, the young people should be able to:

- Describe the experience of being signed with the cross and called by name.
- Retell and share their understanding of God as their shepherd.
- Understand more fully and explain the sacrament of Baptism as a celebration of our sharing in God's life.
- Appreciate what being a child of God means for their lives.
- Choose to make a difference by doing something that shows they trust in God's love.

ENRICHING

These are some additional resources for enhancing the presentation of chapter 1 and for helping families participate in the preparation of their children for the sacrament of Reconciliation:

- RCL's *Reconciliation* music CD, Song 1, "Like a Shepherd"; Song 2, "The Good Shepherd"; Song 3, "El Buen Pastor"; Song 4, "We Are Yours, O Lord"
- RCL's *Reconciliation Family Guide,* pages 16–19
- Scripture play "The Lost Sheep"
- **Videos**
  - **Faith First** Grade 2 video, Segment 6, The Visual Bible™, "The Lost Sheep."
  - **Faith First** Grade 3 video, Segment 2, The Visual Bible™, "The Baptism of Jesus."

MATERIALS NEEDED

Prior to meeting with the young people gather these and any other materials you might need:

- Handouts for chapter 1, one set for each child
- Large, clear glass bowl of water
- Recording of instrumental music, and lyrics and music for a hymn related to the theme of the opening ritual
- Bible
- Pencils, and crayons or markers
- Scripture card "God Loves Us," one for each child

 Visit the RCL sacraments web site by following the link titled "Sacraments" at www.FaithFirst.com.

Blessing with Water

Gathering

Gather the young people around the baptismal font for this prayer ritual. Play a recording of instrumental music or an appropriate hymn. Invite the participants to settle themselves and to become aware of God's presence.

Alternative: Gather the young people in the prayer area. In the center of the area place a table and on the table place a large bowl of water. Play a recording of instrumental music or an appropriate hymn. Invite the participants to settle themselves and to become aware of God's presence.

LEADER: Let us begin by praying the Sign of the Cross to remind us of our baptism.

ALL: *Make the sign of the cross, saying,*
In the name of the Father,
and of the Son,
and of the Holy Spirit. Amen.

LEADER: Loving God, our Creator,
you are with us as we gather in prayer.
Open our hearts to your word.
We ask this in the name of your Son,
    Jesus Christ.

ALL: Amen.

Scripture Reading

Proclaim or invite a volunteer to proclaim from the Bible Luke 15:1–7, the parable of the lost sheep.

LEADER: Let us make the sign of a cross on our forehead, lips, and over our heart and ask the Holy Spirit to help us listen to the word of God.

We Belong to God — CHAPTER 1
Opening Ritual

READER: A reading from the holy gospel according to Luke.

ALL: *Reverently sign their forehead, lips, and over their heart with the sign of the cross and then say,*
Glory to you, Lord.

READER: *Proclaim Luke 15:1–7. Conclude the reading, saying,*
The gospel of the Lord.

ALL: Praise to you, Lord Jesus Christ.

Ritual: Signing with Water

LEADER: *Play a recording of appropriate instrumental music or an appropriate hymn. Invite the young people to come forward one at a time. Dip your hand in the water and mark each child's forehead with the sign of the cross. Address each child by name and say,*
(Name), you belong to Christ. In the name of the Father, and of the Son, and of the Holy Spirit.

CHILD: Amen.

Closing Prayer

LEADER: Loving God, Creator and Father,
you call us by name;
we belong to you.
We thank you for the gift of water
that reminds us that you share your life
    and love with us.
Help us live as children of God.
We ask this through Jesus Christ our Lord.

ALL: Amen.

Opening Ritual

Objective

Experience the ritual action of being called by name and blessed with water and reflect on the experience.

Introduce

- Introduce yourself to the group.
- Invite the young people to introduce themselves to one another. For example, use a brief icebreaker activity or simply have each person state their name and if they wish, add a brief statement that describes something positive about themselves.
- Give a brief overview of what will be happening during the weeks of sacrament preparation.

Celebrate

Celebrate the Ritual

Lead the young people in the celebration of the opening ritual, which is found on page 160.

Reflect

Guide the participants in a reflection on their experience of the opening ritual. Invite responses to the question, What was it like for you to be called by name and blessed with water?

Discover

Facilitate the young peoples' connection of the ritual experience with their daily lives. Invite responses to the question, When are some important times you are called by name?

Apply

Integrate

- Invite volunteers to identify some of the times when they make the sign of the cross.

- Summarize by pointing out that we bless ourselves with holy water as we enter a church. Explain that this reminds us of our Baptism and that we are sons and daughters of God.
- Remind the group that we call God by the name Holy Trinity. Review what we mean when we name God "Trinity"—there is one God in three Persons: God the Father, God the Son, and God the Holy Spirit.

God Loves Us
(Scripture)

Objective

Tell the parable of the lost sheep and reflect on its meaning.

Teach

Connect

Remind the young people that at Baptism the priest or deacon, their parents, and godparents traced a cross on their forehead. This ritual action is a sign that they belong to God in a very special way.

Discover

- Present and discuss the section "Bible Background." Use the "Think About It" questions to lead the discussion.
- Point out that throughout the Bible, God is often described as the shepherd of his people. Then invite a volunteer to read aloud the parable of the Good Shepherd found in Luke 15:4–6.

Reflect

After a moment of reflection, read the "Faith Focus" question aloud and invite responses. Invite everyone to imagine that they are lost and to visualize what it would be like to be found by a caring and loving person. If journal writing is part of your process, have the young people describe their experience in their journals.

Apply
Integrate

- Distribute the handouts for chapter 1, "We Belong to God." Turn to the handout "God Loves Us" and work in small groups to read and discuss "Understanding the Word of God," using the question, What does it mean to call God our shepherd? Invite each group to share its responses.

- Explain that we are lost when we choose not to listen to God and not to do what we know God wants us to do. Remind the young people of God's unconditional love for each of us. Guide the young people in trusting more deeply God's love for each of them.

At Home

Encourage the young people to share what they have learned with their families.

LESSON PLAN

Jesus, the Good Shepherd
(Doctrine/Liturgy)

Objective
Help the group discover that Baptism makes us sharers in God's love and life.

Teach
Connect

Recall the parable of the good shepherd. Ask and discuss what that parable tells us about God.

Discover

- Turn to the handout "Jesus, the Good Shepherd" and present the first paragraph.

- Remind them that one of the titles of Jesus is the Good Shepherd. Invite several volunteers to read about Jesus the Good Shepherd in John 10:1–18. Summarize by reading aloud the section "The Good Shepherd."

- Present the sections "Marked with the Sign of the Good Shepherd" and "Our Baptism." Use the "Think About It" questions to process the material.

- Emphasize that at Baptism we share in the death and resurrection of Jesus. Our sins are forgiven. We are reborn to new life in Christ. We receive the promise of eternal life in heaven.

- Share "What We See and Hear." Tell the young people that the priest also blesses us with the sign of the cross in the sacrament of Reconciliation.

Reflect

Discuss what it means to them to belong to God forever. If journal writing is part of your process, have the young people record their reflections in their journals.

Apply
Integrate

Recall the importance of the sign of the cross and that each of us was marked with the sign of the cross when we were baptized. Invite everyone to stand and to slowly and reverently pray the Sign of the Cross.

At Home

Encourage the young people to share what they have learned with their families.

LESSON PLAN

What Difference Does This Make in My Life?/ Together as a Family

Objective

Decide to put our faith into action and make a difference.

Connect

Summarize

Recall that the story of the good shepherd is a story about God's love for us. God shares his love for us in a special way at Baptism.

Reflect

Share some examples of how parents and grandparents, teachers, and other people in the Church are signs of God's love.

Respond

Discover

Turn to the "What Difference Does This Make in My Life?" handout. Lead the group in a prayer to the Holy Spirit. Invite them to complete the activity.

Choose

● Explain the faith decision activity. Invite the young people to quietly read it and think about how they might complete the faith decision activity.

● Expand the faith decision activity by brainstorming what the whole class or groups of several members of the class can do together to show God's love for people.

Together as a Family

At Home

Distribute copies of the handout "Together as a Family." Invite the young people to share the page with their families.

Sending Forth Ritual

Bless the young people and send them forth to love and serve God and other people. Use this or a similar sending forth rite:

Play the recording of the instrumental version of an appropriate hymn from RCL's Reconciliation music CD. Then invite everyone to gather in the prayer area. Group the young people with partners. Make sure that you also have a partner. Once the group is settled, begin the ritual.

ALL: *Make the sign of the cross, saying,*
In the name of the Father, and of the Son, and of the Holy Spirit. Amen.

LEADER: We are followers of Jesus the Good Shepherd. At Baptism we were marked with the sign of the cross. This shows that we belong to Christ and share in Christ's suffering, death, resurrection, and ascension. Let us turn and face our partner, making the sign of the cross on their forehead as we say our partner's name and then the words "You belong to Jesus the Good Shepherd."

LEADER: *Ask God's blessing on the group, using these or similar words:*
May the blessing of God, our
    Shepherd, be with you.
All bless themselves as you continue:
In the name of the Father,
    and of the Son,
    and of the Holy Spirit.
Go in peace and tell others
    about God's love.

ALL: Thanks be to God.

We Follow Jesus

Background

Love: The Heart of God's Law

In his discourse to the disciples at the Last Supper (John 14–16) Jesus summarized the way of life his disciples were to live. Jesus' command was very clear: Love one another as he had loved them. They were to show their love for him by keeping his commandments. Living such a life was a sign of the indwelling, or presence of God—Father, Son, and Spirit—with them (see John 14).

Love is the center of the life of God. It is also the heart and foundation of human life (see 1 John 4:7–12). This should come as no surprise. Human beings, created in the image and likeness of God—who is love (see 1 John 4:16)—share in the very life and love of God. The divine command to love is at the heart of God's Law.

In the Old Testament the revelation of the Law is summarized in the Shema (see Deuteronomy 6:4–9, 11:13–21; Numbers 15:37–41). When Jesus was asked by the scribe which of the commandments was the greatest, he succinctly reminded the teacher of the Law what he already should have known: living the law of love, as witnessed by one's fidelity to the Covenant, is the source and foundation of holiness. It is the foundational behavior of living as a child of God.

More background: For further reading and reflection see *Catechism of the Catholic Church* 1420–1429, 1730–1742, 1776–1794, 1846–1851, 2013–2014, and 2052–2074.

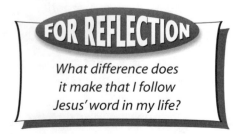

FOR REFLECTION

What difference does it make that I follow Jesus' word in my life?

First Thoughts

Reverence

Reverence, one of the seven Gifts of the Holy Spirit, shapes our attitude of respect not only for God but for all created life. Find ways for the young people to discover that all created life, especially human life, is sacred. Help the young people develop a sense of reverence for one another as images of God. Having such a reverence for themselves is the foundation for true self-love (and self-respect). It is on this foundation that children can truly learn to love others as they love themselves. If the young people exhibit a lack of reverence and respect for one another in the classroom, invite them to rethink their behavior. Remind them of the Great Commandment. Pray with them to the Holy Spirit for help in making better decisions.

Mistakes and Accidents

What are adult responses to the mistakes and accidents caused by children? Sometimes adults react, rather than respond, to such accidents and mistakes as if they were deliberate, consciously chosen harmful behaviors. It is important that we respond appropriately to children who accidentally break an object, run into and knock down another person, spill water, and so on. Our response assuredly will involve the children's learning from such accidents and mistakes by acknowledging the causes, accepting responsibility for the consequences, and making appropriate amends (for example, cleaning up).

Overview

FAITH FOCUS

The Great Commandment is the summary and the heart of all of God's commandments.

OBJECTIVES

After completing the chapter, the young people should be able to:

- Describe the experience of the ritual action of reverently listening to the word of God.
- Retell and share their understanding of the meaning of the Scripture story "The Great Commandment."
- Understand more fully and explain the role of the sacrament of Reconciliation in living the Great Commandment.
- Appreciate the difference that living the Great Commandment means for their lives and the lives of other people.
- Choose to do things that show they are living the Great Commandment.

ENRICHING

These are some additional resources for enhancing the presentation of chapter 2 and for helping families participate in the preparation of their children for the sacrament of Reconciliation:

- RCL's *Reconciliation* music CD, Song 5, "Pescador De Hombres/Lord, You Have Come"; Song 6, "I Have Loved You"
- RCL's *Reconciliation Family Guide,* pages 20–23
- Scripture play "The Great Commandment"
- **Video**
  - **Faith First** Grade 4 video, Segment 4, "Moral Dilemma."

MATERIALS NEEDED

Prior to meeting with the young people gather these and other materials that you might need:

- Handouts for chapter 2, one set for each child
- Recording of instrumental music, and lyrics and music for a hymn related to the theme of the opening ritual
- Bible
- Pencils and crayons or markers
- Poster board or newsprint
- Scripture card "The Great Commandment," one for each child

 Visit the RCL sacraments web site by following the link titled "Sacraments" at www.FaithFirst.com.

Note: The lesson plan begins on page 167.
Celebrate the ritual when indicated.

We Follow Jesus **CHAPTER 2**
Opening Ritual

Reverence for the Word of God

Gathering

Play a recording of instrumental music or an appropriate hymn. Reverently hold a Bible (or the Book of the Gospels if available) in your hands at about eye level. As you process around the room, invite the young people to process silently behind you to the prayer area. Upon arrival at the prayer area, invite everyone to settle themselves and to become aware of God's presence.

Alternative 1: Reverently place the Bible (or the Book of the Gospels) in the prayer area. Invite everyone to come forward and gather around the Scriptures. After they have gathered, invite them to settle themselves and to become aware of God's presence.

Alternative 2: Invite the young people to process from your room to an area in the church or chapel. Reverently hold the Bible in your hands at eye level and lead the participants in the procession into the church or chapel.

LEADER: Let us begin by praying the Sign of the Cross to remind us of our baptism.

ALL: In the name of the Father,
and of the Son,
and of the Holy Spirit. Amen.

LEADER: God, our loving Father,
we gather around your word to us,
the Sacred Scriptures.
Prepare our minds and hearts
to listen to your word.
We ask this through Jesus Christ our Lord.

ALL: Amen.

Scripture Reading

Proclaim or invite a volunteer to proclaim Matthew 22:34–40 from the Bible.

LEADER: Let us make the sign of the cross on our forehead, lips, and over our heart and ask the Holy Spirit to help us listen to the word of God.

READER: A reading from the holy gospel according to Matthew.

ALL: *Reverently sign their forehead, lips, and over their heart with the sign of the cross and then say,*
Glory to you, Lord.

READER: *Proclaim Matthew 22:34–40. Conclude the reading, saying,*
The gospel of the Lord.

ALL: Praise to you, Lord Jesus Christ.

Ritual

Play the instrumental or vocal version of the music used for the gathering procession. Then invite the young people to come forward one at a time to reverence the Bible (or the Book of the Gospels). For example, they may reverently touch or kiss the book.

Closing

LEADER: God, our loving Father,
today we show our reverence
for your word, the Sacred Scriptures.
Send us the Holy Spirit
to help us remember
and follow your word every day.
We ask this through Christ our Lord.

ALL: Amen.

LESSON PLAN
Opening Ritual

Objective
Experience the ritual action of processing with and reverencing the Bible and reflect on its meaning.

Celebrate
Celebrate the Ritual

Lead the young people in the celebration of the opening ritual, which is found on page 166.

Reflect

Guide everyone in a reflection on their experience of the opening ritual. Ask and invite responses to the question, What was it like for you to show reverence for the word of God?

Discover

Facilitate the young people's connection of the ritual showing reverence for the word of God with their daily lives. Invite responses to the question, How do you show reverence at other times?

Apply
Integrate

- Explain that as Catholics we show reverence for the Bible, or Sacred Scripture. This means we show our love and respect for the word of God. Reverence is one of the Gifts of the Holy Spirit that enables us to honor and respect God and all people. Invite volunteers to give one example of how we show reverence for Sacred Scriptures.

- Show and talk about the Book of the Gospels if it was used in the opening ritual. Explain that the Book of the Gospels is carried in procession at the beginning of Mass. It contains the gospel readings that the priest or deacon proclaims both at Mass and at the communal celebration of Reconciliation. We show our reverence for God's word by standing and making the sign of the cross on our forehead, lips, and over our heart before we listen to the gospel reading.

LESSON PLAN
The Great Commandment
(Scripture)

Objective
Tell the Scripture story about the Great Commandment and reflect on its meaning.

Teach
Connect

Recall the experience of showing reverence for the Bible.

Discover

- Distribute the handouts for chapter 2, "We Follow Jesus." Present and discuss the "Bible Background" section on the first handout. Use the "Think About It" question to lead the discussion.

- Invite a volunteer to proclaim Matthew 22:34–40. Invite everyone to discover what Jesus said about the laws, or commandments, that God had given to the Israelites.

- Discuss the Scripture reading, using the "Think About It" question in the section "Reading the Word of God."

Reflect

- Invite everyone to reflect on the reading. After a moment of quiet reflection, ask and discuss: What does the Great Commandment teach? If journal writing is part of your process, have the young people record their reflections in their journals.

- Present the section "Understanding the Word of God." Explain that Jesus' reply to the scribe reminded the inquiring scribe that he should already have known the answer to his own question. Jesus restated the ancient Jewish profession of faith, the Shema (Deuteronomy 6:4–9, 11:13–21; Numbers 15:37–41). The Shema summarized the Law for the Israelites and was recited twice daily.

Apply

Integrate

- Have the young people work in small groups to discuss the "Think About It" question in the section "Understanding the Word of God." Invite each group to share its responses.

- Help everyone understand that our love for God and our love for ourselves and other people are connected. Use the following activity to help with this discussion. Write the headings "Love God," "Love Yourself," and "Love Your Neighbor" on the board or on newsprint. Invite volunteers to list, under each heading, ways that they can show their love for God, for themselves, and for other people. Encourage the participants to choose one of the ideas listed on the board and do it this week.

At Home

Encourage the young people to share what they have learned with their families.

LESSON PLAN

Living a Holy Life
(Doctrine/Liturgy)

Objective

Explain the role of the sacrament of Reconciliation in living the Great Commandment.

Teach

Connect

Review what the Great Commandment teaches. Summarize the discussion by saying that the Great Commandment tells us that we are to love and respect God, ourselves, and all people.

Discover

- Turn to the handout "Living a Holy Life" and invite responses to the "Faith Focus" question. This will help you assess what the group already knows about the sacrament of Reconciliation.

- Discuss the section "Holiness." Have the young people work with a partner to discuss the meaning of conscience and free will. Use the "Think About It" questions to process the material.

- Explain the importance of forming a good conscience. A well-formed conscience helps us decide correctly whether a choice is in accordance with God's Law or against it. But a well-formed conscience does not just happen. It needs to be developed. Here are a few things that can be done to develop a good, or well-formed, conscience: (1) Read and listen to God's word, the Scriptures. (2) Examine the choices Jesus made. (3) Study the teachings of the Church and learn from the example of the saints. (4) Ask the Holy Spirit for understanding, courage, and wisdom. (5) Take part in the celebration of the Eucharist and receive Holy Communion regularly. (6) Celebrate Reconciliation regularly. (7) Seek the advice of a wise spiritual director or companion.

- Present the section "The Sacrament of Penance." Help the group discover the connection between living a holy life and the sacrament of Reconciliation.

- Emphasize the difference between a sin, a mistake, and an accident.

Reflect

Discuss the "Think About It" questions at the bottom of the handout. If journal writing is part of your process, have the young people write their responses to the questions in their journals.

Apply

Integrate

- Help the young people understand that in the sacrament of Penance not only are we forgiven our sins but we also receive the grace to grow as children of God and live holy lives.

- Present the section "What We See and Hear." Explain that Jesus lived the Great Commandment.

- If time permits, have the participants work in groups of three or four to create skits that show how they can live the Great Commandment either at home or in school.

At Home

Encourage the young people to share what they have learned with their families.

What Difference Does This Make in My Life?/ Together as a Family

Objective
Decide to put our faith into action and make a difference.

Connect
Summarize

Recall the two parts of the Great Commandment: Love God with all your heart, soul, and mind; love others as you love yourself. Emphasize that as followers of Jesus we are called to live the Great Commandment.

Reflect

Share examples of ordinary people who serve the community, for example, firefighters and teachers. Point out how the Holy Spirit helps people live the Great Commandment through their daily work.

Respond
Discover

Have the young people turn to the "What Difference Does This Make in My Life?" handout. Invite them to think about ways they might live the Great Commandment. Have them complete the activity.

Choose

● Explain the faith decision activity. Invite the young people to quietly read it and think about how they might complete the faith decision activity.

● Expand the faith decision activity by inviting the participants to work together on a cooperative learning project. Cooperative learning projects can model living the Great Commandment. Young people can show their love for God by acknowledging that their own talents and the talents of others in the group are gifts from God (love of God). They can also express their love for self by recognizing their talents, and their love for others by respectfully inviting others to share their talents by working with one another to complete the project. Invite the participants to create a banner or mural that depicts people of all ages living the Great Commandment. Provide art materials for the young people to create this poster or mural. Encourage a respectful sharing of ideas as they work together.

Together as a Family
At Home

Distribute copies of the handout "Together as a Family." Invite the young people to share the page with their families.

Sending Forth Ritual

Play the recording of the instrumental version of an appropriate hymn from RCL's Reconciliation music CD. Then invite the group to gather in the prayer area. Once they are settled, begin the ritual.

ALL: In the name of the Father, and of the Son, and of the Holy Spirit. Amen.

LEADER: May the Lord guide your hearts in the way of his love and fill you with Christ-like patience.

ALL: Amen.

LEADER: Go in peace.

ALL: Thanks be to God.

We Listen to the Holy Spirit

Background

Life in the Spirit

At Baptism we are reconciled both with God and with the People of God. We are joined to Christ and made sharers in his Paschal mystery, in the saving work of Christ. We are made sharers in the life of the Holy Trinity. We become adopted sons and daughters of God the Father. We receive the grace of the Holy Spirit to live holy lives. Growing in holiness is a cooperative effort. It begins with God showering us with the grace of the Holy Spirit and is followed by our grace-filled, free response to the Holy Spirit. With the grace of the Holy Spirit, we grow in our ability to understand the meaning of our faith and to live by its teachings.

The Holy Spirit gifts us with the courage to overcome obstacles that stand in our way of loving God and others, and with the wisdom to value God above all creatures. The Holy Spirit invites us and strengthens us to use the gift of freedom responsibly and to grow in holiness—in our lives as children of God and the People of God. The Holy Spirit enlightens us with the knowledge of what is right and what is wrong, and urges us to deepen the reconciliation with God and with one another that Christ has established through his death and resurrection. In gratitude we pray: "Lord, by your cross and resurrection you have set us free. You are the Savior of the world" ("Memorial Acclamation," *Roman Missal*).

More background: For further reading and reflection see *Catechism of the Catholic Church* 683–686, 733–741, and 1830–1832.

FOR REFLECTION

What difference does it make when I listen to the Holy Spirit?

First Thoughts

Sacred Space

Our catechetical learning environment is a sacred place. It is the dwelling place of the Holy Spirit who invites everyone—catechist and young people —to cooperate in the work of growing in the love of God, others, and oneself. Living the Great Commandment is the heart of both the Old Law and the New Law; it is also the heart of our ministry with the young people. We need to pause and reflect before and after our time with the group on our classroom-management techniques and strategies. The tone and volume of our voice, the sound of our silence, the look on our face, the movement of our hands, and so many other seemingly small details can reinforce (or undo) our teaching on the value of living the Great Commandment.

The Art of Conversation

Conversation brings people together. True conversation is not a monologue. It is not simply talking to someone. True conversation is talking with someone, a sharing of oneself through speaking and listening. Talkers who do not listen cannot have a true conversation. Talkers who do not listen often make poor or bad decisions because they think that they have all the answers. They seem to be deaf to any point of view but their own. Value your teaching time with the young people as a time for true conversation with them. Listen attentively. Respect the points of view of the participants. Factor their opinions and points of view into your decisions. Model the role and value of listening for making good decisions.

© RCL • Resource for Christian Living®

Overview

FAITH FOCUS

The Holy Spirit helps us make good decisions and put them into action.

OBJECTIVES

After completing this chapter, the young people should be able to:

- Describe the ritual action of lighting candles and what it was like for them to take part in the ritual.
- Retell and share their understanding of the meaning of the Scripture story "The Good Samaritan."
- Understand the nature of sin and explain the rite of confessing our sins to the priest in Reconciliation.
- Appreciate the difference that the sacrament of Reconciliation makes in helping us make better decisions and live as children of God.
- Choose to make a difference by helping someone in need as the good Samaritan helped the injured man.

ENRICHING

These are additional resources for enhancing the presentation of chapter 3 and for helping families participate in the preparation of their children for the sacrament of Reconciliation:

- RCL's *Reconciliation* music CD, Song 7, "Envía Tu Espíritu"; Song 8, "Jesus, Come to Us"; Song 9, "Listen to Jesus"; Song 10, "If Today You Hear God's Voice"
- RCL's *Reconciliation Family Guide,* pages 24–27
- Scripture play "The Good Samaritan"

MATERIALS NEEDED

Prior to meeting with the young people gather these and any other materials you might need:

- Handouts for chapter 3, one set for each child
- Recording of instrumental music, and lyrics and music for a hymn related to the theme of the opening ritual
- Bible
- Pencils and crayons or markers
- Scripture card "The Good Samaritan," one for each child

 Visit the RCL sacraments web site by following the link titled "Sacraments" at www.FaithFirst.com.

Jesus, Light of the World

Gathering

Gather the young people in the church around the Easter candle. Play a recording of instrumental music or an appropriate hymn. Invite everyone to settle themselves and to become aware of God's presence.

Alternative: Gather the young people around a large candle in the prayer area. Play a recording of instrumental music or an appropriate hymn. Invite everyone to settle themselves and to become aware of God's presence.

LEADER: Let us begin by praying the Sign of the Cross to remind us of our baptism.

ALL: *Make the sign of the cross, saying,*
In the name of the Father,
and of the Son,
and of the Holy Spirit. Amen.

LEADER: God of goodness and mercy,
you send us the gift of the Holy Spirit.
Open our minds and hearts to the
Holy Spirit,
who is our teacher and helper.
We ask this in the name of Jesus Christ
our Lord.

ALL: Amen.

Scripture Reading

Proclaim or invite a volunteer to proclaim Luke 10:29–37, the parable of the Good Samaritan.

LEADER: Let us make the sign of the cross on our forehead, lips, and over our heart and ask the Holy Spirit to help us listen to the word of God with reverence.

READER: A reading from the holy gospel according to Luke.

ALL: *Reverently make the sign of the cross on their forehead, lips, and over their heart and then say,*
Glory to you, Lord.

READER: Proclaim Luke 10:29–37. Conclude the reading, saying,
The gospel of the Lord.

ALL: Praise to you, Lord Jesus Christ.

Ritual

ALL: *Gather around the Easter candle. Light the candle, saying,*
Jesus is the Light of the World.

LEADER: *Tell the young people,*
Jesus asked us to be lights in our world.
Ask the young people to name things that the Holy Spirit can help them do to be lights in the world. For example,
Be kind to others.
Listen attentively to my parents.

ALL: *After each statement, respond,*
Jesus, Light of the World,
help us to be lights in the world.

Closing

LEADER: God of goodness and mercy,
thank you for the gift of the Holy Spirit.
Send us the Holy Spirit
to help us live as lights in the world.
We ask this through Jesus Christ our Lord.

ALL: Amen.

LESSON PLAN
Opening Ritual

Objective
Experience the ritual action of lighting candles and reflect on its meaning.

Celebrate
Celebrate the Ritual

Lead the group in the celebration of the opening ritual, which is found on page 172.

Reflect

Guide everyone in a reflection on their experience of the opening ritual. Ask and invite responses to the question, What was it like for you to pray around the lighted candle?

Discover

Facilitate the young people's connection of the ritual experience to their life experience. Ask and invite responses to the question, When does your family use lighted candles?

Apply
Integrate

- Explain that as Catholics we use lighted candles to remind us that Jesus is the Light of the World. Ask volunteers to share one example of when we use lighted candles in church.

- Explain that one of the most important uses of candles is the Church's use of the Easter candle. The Easter candle symbolizes the Risen Jesus, the Light of the World. Blessed and lighted from the new fire at the Easter Vigil, the Easter candle is carried in procession into the darkened church. Three times the deacon or other minister, carrying the candle, proclaims, "Christ our light." Three times the assembly responds, "Thanks be to God." After each proclamation and response, more and more candles held by the ministers and all the members of the assembly are lighted from the flame of the Easter candle. Then, in the church lighted only with the candles, the Easter proclamation, the joyful proclamation of the story of salvation, is retold in song. The same Easter candle, lighted at the Easter Vigil, stands near the baptismal pool or font throughout the year. Each newly baptized person receives a candle lighted from the Easter candle, as the celebrant says, "Receive the light of Christ." The newly baptized have been enlightened by Christ and are "to walk always as children of the light" (*Rite of Baptism for Children* 64).

LESSON PLAN
The Good Samaritan
(Scripture)

Objective
Tell the gospel story of the Good Samaritan and reflect on its meaning.

Teach
Connect

Recall the opening ritual and that Jesus called all his followers to be lights (live "as children of the light") in the world.

Discover

- Distribute the handout "The Good Samaritan" and explain what a parable is, using the "Bible Background" section.

- Discuss some of the other parables that they may recall that Jesus told.

- Ask a volunteer to proclaim the parable of the Good Samaritan found in Luke 10:29–37. Another way to present this parable is to have the young people role-play the story of the Good Samaritan. Divide the class into several groups. Assign members of each group the roles of the robbers, the injured man, the two travelers who did not stop to help, the Samaritan, and the innkeeper.

Ask them to read the story and practice their roles. Invite each group to present its role-play.

● Discuss the Scripture reading using the "Think About It" questions in the section "Reading the Word of God."

Reflect

Invite everyone to reflect on the reading. After a moment of quiet reflection, discuss what the good Samaritan chose to do in the story. If journal writing is part of your process, have the young people record their reflections in their journals.

Apply
Integrate

● Present the section "Understanding the Word of God." Explain that the Samaritans were often viewed as lesser than "a true Israelite." But it is the Samaritan—not the priest or Levite—who witnesses to what it means to live the Covenant and to be a true descendant of Abraham.

● Invite each young person to work with a partner to discuss the "Think About It" questions in the section "Understanding the Word of God." After each pair of children has had time to discuss their responses, summarize by presenting the closing paragraph in the section.

At Home

Encourage the young people to share what they have learned with their families.

LESSON PLAN

We Make Good Decisions
(Doctrine/Liturgy)

Objective
Explain the importance of making good decisions and the rite of the confession of sins.

Teach
Connect

Recall the parable of the Good Samaritan. Remind the young people that the Samaritan made a good decision. He chose to stop and help the injured traveler.

Discover

● Distribute the handout "We Make Good Decisions." Discuss the importance of making good decisions. Invite several volunteers to explain some of the things, which are listed in the section "Making Good Decisions," that can be done to help us learn to make good decisions.

● Have the young people work in small groups to discuss the "Think About It" questions that conclude the section "Making Good Decisions." Invite each group to share with the entire group one of the things that was discussed.

● Present the section "Sin: A Bad Decision" and explain mortal and venial sin. Discuss why sin is a bad decision.

● Connect the concept of sin to the confession of sins in the sacrament of Reconciliation by presenting the sections "Sacrament of Confession" and "Sacrament of Conversion."

● Present "What We See and Hear" to help the young people understand the confession of sins.

Reflect

Ask and discuss the "Think About It" question at the bottom of the handout. If journal writing is part of your process, have the young people write their responses to the questions in their journals.

Apply
Integrate

● Discuss the meaning of responsibility with the young people. Explain that when they say or do things that hurt others, responsible people do not blame others but accept responsibility for their words and actions. Explain that when we confess our sins in the sacrament of Reconciliation, we are taking responsibility for our sins.

● Explain that Reconciliation and Anointing of the Sick are the two Sacraments of Healing celebrated by the Church. Reconciliation continues Baptism's work of forgiveness and conversion. That is why this sacrament is also called the sacrament of conversion. Through the sacrament of Reconciliation we receive the forgiveness of sins committed after Baptism, the grace to live as children of God, and the strength to serve God and neighbor as Jesus taught (*Rite of Penance* 7).

At Home

Encourage the young people to share what they have learned with their families.

© RCL · Resources for Christian Living®

LESSON PLAN

What Difference Does This Make in My Life?/ Together as a Family

Objective
Decide to put our faith into action and make a difference.

Connect

Summarize

Recall the parable of the Good Samaritan from the Bible. Talk about the connection between making good choices and living as lights in the world.

Reflect

Share examples of people, like Mother Teresa of Calcutta, who chose to help the poor and live as a light in the world. Point out that the Holy Spirit helps us to make decisions to show our love for God and for others.

Respond

Discover

Distribute the handout "What Difference Does This Make in My Life?" Invite the young people to work in small groups to complete the activity. When all are finished, have them share their completed work with the entire group.

Choose

● Explain the faith decision activity. Invite the participants to quietly read it and think about how they might complete the faith decision activity.

● Expand the faith decision activity by brainstorming what the whole class or groups of several members of the class can do together to show they are living as a light in the world.

Together as a Family

At Home

Distribute copies of the handout "Together as a Family." Invite the young people to share the page with their families

Sending Forth Ritual

Play the recording of the instrumental version of an appropriate hymn from RCL's Reconciliation music CD. Then invite the group to gather in the prayer area. Once they are settled, begin the ritual.

ALL: In the name of the Father, and of the Son, and of the Holy Spirit. Amen.

LEADER: Holy Spirit,
you are our teacher and helper.
Open our minds and hearts to listen to you.
Help us to make decisions to live
as children of the light.

ALL: Blessed be God for ever.

LEADER: Go in peace. Live as children of the light.

ALL: Blessed be God for ever.

We Are Sorry

Background

Conversion of Heart

The Christian life is a life of continuing conversion to Christ through sharing in his Paschal mystery. We are made sharers in this great mystery of God's love, which Pope John Paul II calls "the mystery of mercy," through the celebration of the sacraments.

Baptism joins us to Christ and establishes us in a new relationship with God the Father, the Son, and the Holy Spirit. All that has separated us from God—original sin and personal sins—is forgiven. We are reconciled, or made one again, with God and with one another.

Living our life in Christ is no easy task. It demands a continuing conversion of heart, a life of penance, with hope in God's mercy and trust in his grace. The Eucharist strengthens our lifelong conversion to Christ, nourishing us to live the gift of life in Christ that we received at Baptism. If we choose to turn our backs on God's love after Baptism, the Holy Spirit invites us to open our hearts, turn back toward God, and be reconciled to God (see 2 Corinthians 5:20).

Through the sacrament of Penance, which is also called the sacrament of conversion, we receive the grace to begin anew, and our communion with God and the Church is restored and strengthened.

More background: For further reading and reflection see *Catechism of the Catholic Church* 599–618, 651–655, 1115, 1407, 1425–1439, 1451–1453, and 1459–1460.

FOR REFLECTION

Where in my life is there a need for conversion?

First Thoughts

Trust and Compassion

The gospel story of Jesus and the children (Mark 10:13–16) models for us a wonderful approach to youth. In his dealings with people, Jesus revealed that we can and should approach God as "Abba" with trust and share everything about ourselves with God—even the acknowledgment of our most serious sins—without fear. Hardness of heart toward those who turn away from his love is not one of the attributes of God.

Actions Speak Louder than Words

The adage "Actions speak louder than words" gives us an insight into the meaning of being truly sorry for our sins. Help the young people see that while sometimes it might be enough to say "I'm sorry," at other times adding a simple gesture or act of kindness is necessary to help heal the harm their actions may have caused to their relationships with others. It is important that you help the young people understand that, at times, simply telling someone "I'm sorry" falls far short of the mark. Everyone needs to learn that they have the responsibility to do something to repair the damage and harm their actions have caused. Use whatever opportunities arise during your time with the young people to help them learn this important dimension of reconciliation.

Overview

FAITH FOCUS

The prayer of sorrow (or act of contrition) and penance express our decision and desire to heal the harm we cause by our sins and to be reconciled with God and the Church.

OBJECTIVES

After completing this chapter, the young people should be able to:

● Describe what the experience of praying the Our Father together was like for them.

● Retell and share their understanding of the meaning of the gospel story of Zacchaeus.

● Explain what it means to be truly sorry for one's sins.

● Appreciate the difference that expressing sorrow makes for living as children of God.

● Choose to make a difference by doing or saying something that shows they are truly sorry.

ENRICHING

These are additional resources for enhancing the presentation of chapter 4 and for helping families participate in the preparation of their children for the sacrament of Reconciliation:

● RCL's *Reconciliation* music CD, Song 11, "Change Our Hearts"; Song 12, "Give Me a New Heart"; Song 13, "I'm Sorry"; Song 14, "Lo siento"

● RCL's *Reconciliation Family Guide*, pages 28–31

● Scripture play "Zacchaeus"

MATERIALS NEEDED

Prior to meeting with the young people gather these and any other materials you might need:

● Handouts for chapter 4, one set for each child

● Recording of instrumental music, and lyrics and music for a hymn related to the theme of the opening ritual

● Bible

● Pencils and crayons or markers

● Scripture card "Zacchaeus," one for each child

 Visit the RCL sacraments web site by following the link titled "Sacraments" at www.FaithFirst.com.

© RCL • Resources for Christian Living®

Note: *The lesson plan begins on page 179.*
Celebrate the ritual when indicated.

Praying the Our Father

Gathering

Gather the young people in the prayer area. Play a recording of instrumental music or an appropriate hymn. Invite everyone to settle themselves and to become aware of God's presence. Have everyone recall that Baptism makes us adopted children of God.

LEADER: Let us begin as we were baptized.

ALL: *Make the sign of the cross, saying,*
In the name of the Father,
and of the Son,
and of the Holy Spirit. Amen.

LEADER: Let us pray.
Loving God,
you are our Father.
Help us know and trust your love for us.
Open our hearts to the Holy Spirit.
We ask this in the name of Jesus Christ
     our Lord.

ALL: Amen.

Scripture Reading

Proclaim or invite a volunteer to proclaim Luke 19:1–10, the Scripture story "Zacchaeus," from the Bible.

LEADER: Let us make the sign of the cross on our forehead, lips, and over our heart and ask the Holy Spirit to help us listen to the word of God.

READER: A reading from the holy gospel according to Luke.

ALL: *Reverently make the sign of the cross on their forehead, lips, and over their heart and then say,*
Glory to you, Lord.

READER: Proclaim Luke 19:1–10. Conclude the reading, saying,
The gospel of the Lord.

ALL: Praise to you, Lord Jesus Christ.

Ritual Prayer

Remind the young people that Jesus promised that whenever his disciples gather together he is present with them. Then invite everyone to pray the Our Father.

LEADER: *If you are comfortable doing so, lead the group in praying the Our Father by slightly extending your arms and holding the palms of your hands upward—a traditional gesture of petitioning God and showing our openness to God. Share that this is a sign that we are opening our hearts to God's mercy and love.*
As a sign of our unity and that we are all children of God, let us pray together the prayer that Jesus taught us.

ALL: Our Father, who art in heaven,
hallowed be thy name; thy kingdom come;
thy will be done on earth as it is in heaven.
Give us this day our daily bread;
and forgive us our trespasses
as we forgive those who trespass against us;
and lead us not into temptation,
but deliver us from evil. Amen.

Closing Prayer

LEADER: God, our loving Father,
we gather today to remember your great love for us. Send us the Holy Spirit.
Help us to both forgive and seek forgiveness and to live as your children.
We ask this in the name Jesus Christ our Lord.

ALL: Amen.

LESSON PLAN
Opening Ritual

Objective
Experience the ritual action of praying the Our Father and reflect on its meaning.

Celebrate

Celebrate the Ritual

Lead the group in the celebration of the opening ritual, which is found on page 178.

Reflect

Guide everyone in a reflection on their experience of the opening ritual. Invite responses to the question, What was it like for you to pray the Our Father with our group?

Discover

Facilitate the young people's connection of the ritual experience to their life experience. Ask and invite responses to the question, When do you pray with others?

Apply

Integrate

- Explain that as Catholics we ask God, our loving Father, for forgiveness. We forgive others as God forgives us when we are truly sorry. Ask volunteers to give one example of how we show we are sorry.
- Remind the young people that the Our Father is also called the Lord's Prayer because Jesus gave us this prayer. The Our Father is in some ways a blueprint for living the Gospel. Flowing from Jesus' heart, this prayer expresses the intimacy and communion between Jesus and his Father. By sharing the prayer with us, Jesus invites us to share in that intimacy and communion. When we pray the Our Father we profess our faith and hope in God and his loving plan of creation and salvation. We surrender our hearts to God, petitioning that we share in the love that unites God the Father, the Son, and the Holy Spirit. The ministry of reconciliation—of restoring the communion and intimacy between God and humankind—was the heart of Jesus' ministry on earth, and it is the heart of the Holy Spirit's ministry among us as we prepare for the coming of the kingdom of God. Moved by the Holy Spirit we are called to forgive others generously and joyfully as God forgives us. We are called to live in communion and peace with one another as we desire to live in communion and peace with God now on earth and forever in heaven.
- Summarize by pointing out that when we pray the Our Father, we are telling God how much we trust and love him. We are saying that we want to forgive others as God forgives us.

LESSON PLAN
Zaccheus
(Scripture)

Objective
Tell the gospel story about Zaccheus and reflect on its meaning.

Teach

Connect

Recall with the young people their experience of the ritual of praying the Our Father. Point out that praying the Our Father reminds us that we are called both to seek forgiveness and to forgive.

Discover

- Distribute the handout "We Are Sorry." Present and discuss the section "Bible Background." Invite volunteers to share their responses to the "Think About It" question.
- Point out that the Scripture story for this chapter is a story about a tax collector named Zaccheus.
- Read the "Faith Focus" question aloud and ask the young people to discover the answer as they listen to the Bible story.
- Proclaim the gospel story in Luke 19:1–10, "Zaccheus the Tax Collector." Discover what Zaccheus did to show that he was truly sorry for treating people unfairly.

Reflect

Provide an opportunity for everyone to reflect on the reading. After a moment of quiet reflection, ask, What did Zacchaeus do to make up with the people of Jericho? Invite volunteers to share their insights into the meaning of the Bible story. If journal writing is part of your process, have the young people write their reflections in their journals.

Apply
Integrate

● Have the young people work with a partner to discuss the section "Understanding the Word of God."

● Invite volunteers to share their responses to the "Think About It" question that concludes the section "Understanding the Word of God."

● Explain that the Bible story of Zacchaeus gives us insight into the meaning of the conversion of heart and mind that the Holy Spirit continuously invites us to undergo. It also helps us understand the essential elements of the sacrament of Penance, which are part of the conversion process. Zacchaeus came to know his sin (examination of conscience). He was sorry for treating the people unfairly (contrition). He knew and admitted what he did wrong (confession). He decided to treat people fairly and he showed his decision to change by what he did (penance or satisfaction). He was forgiven and reconciled to God and the people whom he offended by his unjust actions (absolution). He was now recommitted to living the Great Commandment as a true descendant of Abraham (a child of God). Hence Jesus' remark that salvation came to Zacchaeus' house that day.

● If time permits, have volunteers pantomime situations in which they do something to make amends for doing something wrong.

At Home

Encourage the young people to share what they have learned with their families.

LESSON PLAN

We Tell God We Are Sorry
(Doctrine/Liturgy)

Objective
Explain that being sorry for sins and expressing sorrow shows our love for God and others.

Teach
Connect

Recall the story of Zacchaeus. Emphasize that Zacchaeus both felt sorry and showed he was sorry by doing something to heal the harm he caused by deliberately treating people unfairly.

Discover

● Present the opening paragraph on the handout "We Tell God We Are Sorry." Ask and discuss: How is being sorry a sign of love?

● Read aloud the "Faith Focus" question. Invite the young people to work in small groups and discover the answer to the question by discussing the section "The Spirit of Forgiveness."

● Summarize by pointing out that showing sorrow for our sins is one of the important parts of Reconciliation.

Reflect

Guide the young people to reflect on the discussion by using the "Think About It" question at the bottom of the handout. Make sure that they appreciate the importance of contrition (sorrow) and penance (satisfaction), which are essential elements of the celebration of Reconciliation. If journal writing is part of your process, have the young people write their reflections in their journals.

Apply
Integrate

● Present the section "What We See and Hear" and explain the significance of the stole.

- Recall the words "Forgive us our trespasses as we forgive those who trespass against us" that we pray in the Our Father. Point out that we trust God to forgive our sins when we show we are truly sorry. Then explain that people who ask us for forgiveness should also be able to trust that we will forgive them.
- Tell the young people that Jesus called God the Father "Abba." Share with the young people that Jesus told us that we too are to think of God as Abba, a loving parent who loves more than we could ever imagine. Distribute art materials to the children and invite them to create a prayer card. Have them print the words "Abba, God our Father, thank you for loving me so much!" on the prayer card and decorate the prayer card.

At Home

Encourage the young people to share what they have learned with their families.

What Difference Does This Make in My Life?/ Together as a Family

Objective
Decide to put our faith into action and make a difference.

Connect
Summarize

Recall the Bible story of Zacchaeus. Emphasize that Zacchaeus showed that he was sorry for treating the people unfairly. Point out that in the sacrament of Reconciliation we both say that we are sorry and promise to do something to heal the harm we have caused by our sins.

Respond
Reflect

Share the story of Pope John Paul II forgiving the man who tried to kill him. Or share another appropriate story of sorrow and forgiveness that results in reconciliation.

Discover

- Have the young people turn to the "What Difference Does This Make in My Life?" handout. Present the opening paragraph.
- Have everyone read the directions to the activity. Answer any questions about the directions.
- Invite volunteers to share their completed prayer with the entire group.

Choose

- Share the faith decision activity. Invite the young people to think about how they might complete the faith decision activity.
- Expand the faith decision activity by helping everyone appreciate that sometimes a whole group of people offend a person or another group of people. Have the young people name ways a group, like their class, might tell someone or another group they are sorry and want to make up.

Together as a Family
At Home

Have the young people turn to the "Together as a Family" handout. Review the ideas on the page with the group. Encourage the young people to share the page with their families.

Sending Forth Ritual

Play the recording of the instrumental version of an appropriate hymn from RCL's Reconciliation music CD. Then invite the young people to gather in the prayer area. Once they are settled, begin the ritual.

LEADER: May God, our loving Father, fill you with his love.

ALL: Amen.

LEADER: May Jesus help you live as he taught Zacchaeus to live.

ALL: Amen.

LEADER: May the Holy Spirit give you the strength to make up with people whom you have hurt by your words or actions.

ALL: Amen.

LEADER: God, our loving Father, always forgives us our sins. Go in peace.

ALL: Thanks be to God.

We Are Forgiven

Background

The Ministry of Reconciliation

Reconciliation, like sin, affects the entire Body of Christ, the Church. The bishops gathered at the Second Vatican Council wrote: "Those who approach the sacrament of Penance obtain pardon from God's mercy for the offense committed against him, and are, at the same time, reconciled with the Church" (*Dogmatic Constitution on the Church* [Lumen gentium] 11).

While the communal effects of sin and reconciliation may not be as clearly seen in the "Rite for Reconciliation of Individual Penitents," these effects of sin are more clearly expressed in the communal celebration of reconciliation ("Introduction," *Rite of Penance* 22).

In the communal rite all penitents assemble together as the one Body of Christ to seek forgiveness and conversion of heart. Together, the assembly listens to God calling them both as individuals and as a community to conversion and to a renewal of their baptismal commitment to repent and believe in the Gospel. After praying the Lord's Prayer as a community, those who wish meet individually with a priest to confess their sins and receive absolution. The penitents then return to the assembly and praise God. Reconciled to God and to one another, they are sent forth to be living signs of God's love in the world.

More background: For further reading and reflection see *Catechism of the Catholic Church* 1423, 1424, 1440–1449, and 1461–1470.

FOR REFLECTION

What difference does it make that I have asked for forgiveness and have been willing to forgive?

First Thoughts

Acts of Kindness

Teach the young people ways to develop the biblical virtue of kindness (see Micah 6:8). When the need arises to discipline a child firmly, do so fairly with a kind and loving heart. Fill your time together with random acts of kindness. When the young people experience your kindness, it will help them prepare to approach God, a God of mercy and kindness, in the sacrament of Reconciliation with trust. By following your example and living the virtue of kindness themselves, the young people will develop forgiving hearts—hearts that will move them to forgive others as generously and kindly as God forgives them.

The Joy of Forgiveness

One of the most touching parts of the parable of the prodigal son is the father embracing his son when he returns home. The son's heart was filled with sorrow for having "trespassed" against his father. The father, knowing and feeling his son's sorrow, embraces him and welcomes him home unconditionally with a heart filled with joy. Praying the Our Father reminds us of God's forgiving love and our call, as young people of God, to share that forgiving love with others. As the father in the parable of the prodigal son accepted the sorrow of his son and forgave him, we too are to forgive others.

Overview

FAITH FOCUS

In the sacrament of Reconciliation God forgives our sins through the ministry of bishops and priests.

ENRICHING

These are some additional resources for enhancing the presentation of chapter 5 and for helping families participate in the preparation of their children for the sacrament of Reconciliation:

- RCL's *Reconciliation* music CD, Song 15, "God of Mercy"; Song 16, "Be with Me, Lord"
- RCL's *Reconciliation Family Guide*, pages 32–35
- Scripture play "The Forgiving Father"

OBJECTIVES

After completing this chapter, the young people should be able to:

- Describe their experience of the ritual action of the laying on of hands.
- Retell and share their understanding of the meaning of the New Testament story of the forgiving father.
- Explain that we receive forgiveness for our sins in the sacrament of Reconciliation through the ministry of bishops and priests.
- Appreciate the difference that trusting in God's forgiving love makes in their lives.
- Choose to make a difference by forgiving someone.

MATERIALS NEEDED

Prior to meeting with the young people gather these and any other materials you might need:

- Handouts for chapter 5, one set for each child
- Recording of instrumental music, and lyrics and music for a hymn related to the theme of the opening ritual
- Bible
- Pencils and crayons or markers
- Poster board
- Scripture card "The Forgiving Father," one for each child

 Visit the RCL sacraments web site by following the link titled "Sacraments" at www.FaithFirst.com.

Note: *The lesson plan begins on page 185. Celebrate the ritual when indicated.*

Laying On of Hands

Gathering

Gather the young people in the prayer area. Play a recording of instrumental music or an appropriate hymn. Invite everyone to settle themselves and to become aware of God's presence with and among them. Remind everyone that at Baptism they received the gift of the Holy Spirit and the grace to live as young people of God.

LEADER: Invite the young people to pray, saying,
Let us begin as we were baptized.

ALL: *Make the sign of the cross, saying,*
In the name of the Father,
and of the Son,
and of the Holy Spirit. Amen.

LEADER: God, forgiving Father,
Jesus showed us how much you love us.
Send us the Holy Spirit
to help us trust your forgiveness and grace.
Open our hearts to listen to your word.
We ask this through Jesus Christ our Lord.

ALL: Amen.

Scripture Reading

Proclaim or invite a volunteer to proclaim Luke 15:11–32, the parable of the forgiving father, from the Bible.

LEADER: Let us make the sign of the cross on our forehead, lips, and over our heart and ask the Holy Spirit to help us listen to the word of God.

READER: A reading from the holy gospel according to Luke.

ALL: *Reverently make the sign of the cross on their forehead, lips, and over their heart and then say,*
Glory to you, Lord.

READER: *Proclaim Luke 15:11–32. Conclude the reading, saying,*
The gospel of the Lord.

ALL: Praise to you, Lord Jesus Christ.

Ritual Laying On of Hands

LEADER: *Invite the participants to come forward one at a time. Place your open hands on the head of each child, silently pray, and conclude by saying aloud,*
Remember that God always loves you.

CHILD: Thanks be to God.

LEADER: *After you have completed this ritual, say aloud,*
Let us now pray the prayer Jesus taught us.

ALL: Our Father . . .

Closing Prayer

LEADER: *Hold your hands outward, palms down and extended over the young people, and pray,*
God, our forgiving Father,
you always love us.
Send the Holy Spirit of forgiveness upon these young people.
Help them trust in your forgiving love.
Help them share your forgiving love with others.
We ask this in the name of Jesus Christ our Lord.

ALL: Amen.

LESSON PLAN
Opening Ritual

Objective
Experience the ritual action of the laying on of hands and reflect on its meaning.

Celebrate
Celebrate the Ritual

Lead the young people in the celebration of the opening ritual which is found on page 184.

Reflect

Guide the young people in a reflection on their experience of the opening ritual. Invite them to share what it was like for them to experience the ritual of the laying on of hands in the opening prayer celebration.

Discover

Facilitate the young people's connection of the ritual experience to their life experience. Ask and invite responses to the question, What do you do to make up, or reconcile, with others?

Apply
Integrate

- Explain that we all share in God's forgiving love. We make up, or reconcile, with God and with others. Ask volunteers to give one example of how we reconcile with God and with others.
- Connect the reflection on the opening prayer celebration to the sacrament of Reconciliation. Point out that in Reconciliation, the priest will either place his hands on, or hold his hands over, their heads as he prays the words of forgiveness.
- Explain the ancient gesture of the laying on of hands. This gesture is frequently used in both the Old Testament and the New Testament. The gesture of the laying on of hands, which is used widely in the rituals of the Church, has a variety of meanings. In the Scriptures it is most commonly used to invoke God's blessing upon a person or group of people. It is used in a similar way in the

celebration of the sacraments. In Reconciliation this gesture reminds us that the work of forgiveness is indeed the work of the Holy Spirit whom Jesus gave to his disciples as he shared with them the power and ministry of forgiving sins in his name.

LESSON PLAN
The Forgiving Father

Objective
Tell the parable of the forgiving father and reflect on its meaning.

Teach
Connect

Recall the opening ritual. Remind the young people that when we place, or lay, our hands on a person's head during prayer, it is a sign that we are asking God to bless that person.

Discover

- Distribute the handout "We Are Forgiven." Present and discuss the section "Bible Background." Invite volunteers to share their responses to the "Think About It" question.
- Read the "Faith Focus" question aloud and ask the young people to discover the answer as they listen to the parable of the forgiving father.
- Proclaim the gospel story of the forgiving father, found in Luke 15:11–32. Discover what the story teaches us about God's love for us.

Reflect

Provide an opportunity for the young people to reflect on the reading. After a moment of quiet reflection, ask the following questions:

- What did the father do to show that he welcomed his son back home?
- What does this story tell us about God's love for us?

Invite the young people to share their insights into the meaning of the Bible story. If journal writing is part of your process, have the young people write their reflections in their journals.

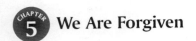

Apply

Integrate

● Invite the young people to discuss the section "Understanding the Word of God" in small groups. Use the "Think About It" questions to summarize the discussion.

● Ask the young people to think about their responses to the "Faith Focus" question. Stress the connection between asking for forgiveness from others and forgiving others.

● Conclude by sharing the last paragraph on the handout.

At Home

Encourage the young people to share what they have learned with their families.

LESSON PLAN

The Gift of Forgiveness
(Doctrine/Liturgy)

Objective

Explain that in the sacrament of Reconciliation our sins are forgiven and we are reconciled with God and with our church family.

Teach

Connect

Recall the parable of the forgiving father. Summarize by reading the section "Forgiveness" aloud to the group.

Discover

● Have the young people work with a partner to discuss the sections "Baptism" and "Eucharist." Conclude the discussion by having the entire group discuss the "Think About It" questions.

● Write the word *absolution* on the board or on newsprint. Explain that absolution is another word for forgiveness. Emphasize that Christ is acting in the sacrament of Reconciliation through the priest.

● Have a volunteer read the "Faith Focus" question aloud. Tell the group to listen for the answer as you present the section "Words of Forgiveness— The Prayer of Absolution."

● Have the young people discuss the "Think About It" question with a partner.

Reflect

Share with the young people the prayer of absolution, or forgiveness, that the priest prays in the sacrament of Reconciliation as he holds his hands over our head. Connect the words and actions of the prayer of absolution with the words and actions of the parable of the forgiving father.

The full prayer of absolution is:

> God, the Father of mercies,
> through the death and resurrection of his Son
> has reconciled the world to himself
> and sent the Holy Spirit among us
> for the forgiveness of sins;
> through the ministry of the Church
> may God give you pardon and peace,
> and I absolve you from your sins
> in the name of the Father,
> and of the Son,
> and of the Holy Spirit. Amen.

Apply

Integrate

● Have the young people read the "Faith Focus" question again, and discuss responses to the question.

● Present the section "What We See and Hear." Recall the importance of the gesture of laying on of hands, which was presented as part of the discussion of the opening ritual.

● Point out that the priest blesses us with the sign of the cross at the end of the prayer of absolution. Explain that the cross is the central symbol that identifies Christians. It captures for us the unconditional love and mercy of God revealed in the death and resurrection of Jesus. Through the sacrifice of Jesus, the Son of God, our sins are forgiven.

● If time permits, have the participants create a reconciliation poster that reinforces their appreciation that we are reconciled with God and with one another in the sacrament of Reconciliation. Distribute art materials, and invite the young people to draw the outline of a large cross on a

© RCL • Resources for Christian Living®

piece of poster board. Have them print the words "Forgiving Father, You Reconcile Us with One Another" on the poster and decorate it.

At Home

Encourage the young people to share what they have learned with their families.

LESSON PLAN

What Difference Does This Make in My Life?/ Together as a Family

Objective
Decide to put our faith into action and make a difference.

Connect
Summarize

Recall what the son in the Bible story did to make up with his father, and what the father did to show he forgave his son. Connect the story with the sacrament of Reconciliation.

Respond
Reflect

Share the story of Saint Paul the Apostle. Tell how he persecuted Christians before he became a follower of Jesus, was forgiven, and told everyone about Jesus and God's forgiving love.

Discover

- Have the group turn to the "What Difference Does This Make in My Life?" handout. Present the opening paragraph.
- Have the young people read the directions to the activity. Answer any questions about the directions.
- Lead the group in a prayer to the Holy Spirit. Then have them complete the activity.
- Emphasize that they may keep their stories of forgiveness confidential, if they wish. You may suggest that the young people write their responses to this activity in their journals, if journal writing is a part of your process.

Choose

- Share the faith decision activity. Invite the young people to think about how they might complete the faith decision activity.
- Brainstorm with the young people different ways that they can show they forgive someone.
- Remind the young people that the Holy Spirit always invites us to forgive others as God forgives us. This is not always easy to do. Sometimes, getting even seems the better choice to make. Emphasize the difference between getting even and forgiving. Summarize the discussion by contrasting the results of getting even and the results of forgiving.

Together as a Family
At Home

Have the young people turn to the "Together as a Family" handout. Review the ideas on the page with the group. Encourage the young people to share the page with their families.

Sending Forth Ritual

Play the recording of the instrumental version of an appropriate hymn from RCL's Reconciliation *music CD. Then invite everyone to gather in the prayer area. Once the young people are settled, begin the ritual.*

LEADER: All-holy Father,
you have given us new life in Jesus, your Son. Send the Holy Spirit to help us live as signs of your love for everyone to see.
ALL: Amen.
LEADER: Bow your heads and ask for God's blessing. May God the Father, the Son, and the Holy Spirit help you to live as Jesus taught.
ALL: Amen.
LEADER: May God fill your heart with kindness to forgive others as he forgives you.
ALL: Amen.
LEADER: May almighty God bless you, the Father, and the Son, and the Holy Spirit.
ALL: Amen.
LEADER: Go in peace.
ALL: Thanks be to God.

CHAPTER 6 · We Are Peacemakers

Background

The Kingdom of Peace

The Father sent his only Son, Jesus, to announce the kingdom of God, to establish peace and the reconciliation of people with God and with all creation. Scripture reveals that peace, or *shalom,* is God's gift to humankind. Making all people sharers in this peace is central to the mission of Jesus, the Prince of Peace (see Luke 2:14, John 20:21). Jesus established this peace through his Paschal mystery (see Luke 19:39).

Jesus shared his work of reconciliation with his disciples. When he sent them out among the people, Jesus gave them the instruction to assess people's readiness to receive them and their message. Jesus told his disciples that when they entered a home, they were to greet people, saying, "Peace to all who live here" (based on Luke 10:5). If the people returned the greeting, the disciples should stay with them and teach them about the kingdom. If not, the disciples were to move on.

All the baptized are anointed to announce the kingdom established by Christ and make all people sharers in the peace of Christ. When we strive to live as peacemakers, we make a difference. We are blessed and bring God's blessings to others (see Matthew 5:9).

More background: For further reading and reflection see *Catechism of the Catholic Church* 736, 1424, 1468, 1716, 1832, 2302, 2305, and 2442.

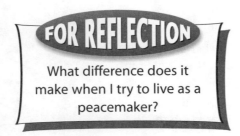

FOR REFLECTION

What difference does it make when I try to live as a peacemaker?

First Thoughts

Peacemakers

Living as peacemakers is not always an easy responsibility to fulfill. What a difference it makes when we face a conflict or violence, step back and gain perspective, control our impulse to get even, and remember that we have been sent by Jesus to be messengers of peace, not violence. At Baptism we are anointed to be messengers of the Prince of Peace, announcing, in word and deed, the kingdom of peace. At Eucharist we are nourished to be messengers of peace and sent forth to love and serve God and one another. Reconciliation also strengthens us to be messengers of Christ's peace. Freed from our sins and reconciled with God and one another, we are sent forth to forgive and reconcile as God has forgiven and reconciled us to himself. We are sent forth to build the kingdom of peace announced by Jesus.

Peaceful Solutions

Conflicts will inevitably arise among the young people. Help the young people solve these conflicts peacefully. When a conflict arises, invite them to stop and take a "peaceful pause." Guide them to discover and work toward a peaceful solution. Use these or similar steps: (1) Pray to the Holy Spirit. (2) Listen attentively and respectfully to one another. (3) Talk with one another and agree on the source of the conflict. (4) Decide on two or three solutions that all agree to use to solve the problem. (5) Implement one of the solutions. (6) If the solution works, celebrate the peaceful working out of the problem. (7) If the solution does not work, have the group try another solution and keep working at solving the problem successfully.

Overview

FAITH FOCUS

The sacrament of Reconciliation makes us sharers in God's gift of peace and renews our calling to share that peace with others.

OBJECTIVES

After completing this chapter, the young people should be able to:
- Describe their experience of sharing peace with others.
- Retell and share their understanding of the meaning of the gospel story recounting Jesus sharing the gift of peace with his disciples.
- Understand and explain that receiving the gift of peace is one of the effects of celebrating Reconciliation.
- Discover and appreciate the difference that peacemakers make for themselves and for other people.
- Choose to make a difference by living as peacemakers.

ENRICHING

These are some additional resources for enhancing the presentation of chapter 6 and for helping families participate in the preparation of their children for the sacrament of Reconciliation:
- RCL's *Reconciliation* music CD, Song 17, "Open My Eyes"; Song 18, "Peace Is Flowing Like a River"
- RCL's *Reconciliation Family Guide*, pages 36–39
- Scripture play "The Gift of Peace"

MATERIALS NEEDED

Prior to meeting with the young people gather these and any other materials you might need:
- Handouts for chapter 6, one set for each child
- Recording of instrumental music, and lyrics and music for a hymn related to the theme of the opening ritual
- Bible
- Pencils, crayons, markers
- Poster board
- Scripture card "The Gift of Peace," one for each child

 Visit the RCL sacraments web site by following the link titled "Sacraments" at www.FaithFirst.com.

Sharing a Sign of Peace

Gathering

Gather the young people in the prayer area. Play a recording of instrumental music or an appropriate hymn. Invite everyone to settle themselves and to become aware of God's presence with and among them. Remind everyone that Baptism makes us followers of Jesus, who taught that young people of God are peacemakers.

LEADER: Let us begin as we were baptized.

ALL: *Make the sign of the cross, saying,*
In the name of the Father,
and of the Son,
and of the Holy Spirit. Amen.

LEADER: God, our loving Father,
you sent us your Son, the Prince of Peace.
Help us know and share the peace
that the Holy Spirit brings us.
Open our hearts to your word
that we may learn to live as peacemakers.
We ask this through Jesus Christ our Lord.

ALL: Amen.

Scripture Reading

Proclaim or invite a volunteer to proclaim John 14:15–27 and 20:21, the story "The Gift of Peace," from the Bible.

LEADER: Let us make the sign of the cross on our forehead, lips, and over our heart and ask the Holy Spirit to help us listen to the word of God.

READER: A reading from the holy gospel according to John.

ALL: Reverently make the sign of the cross on their forehead, lips, and over their heart and then say, Glory to you, Lord.

READER: Proclaim John 14:15–27 and 20:21. Conclude the reading, saying,
The gospel of the Lord.

ALL: Praise to you, Lord Jesus Christ.

Ritual Peace Greeting

LEADER: We are all young people of God.
Let us pray as Jesus taught us:

ALL: Our Father . . .

LEADER: Jesus gave the gift of his peace
to his followers.
Let us share that gift of peace
with one another as Jesus did.

ALL: *Share a sign of peace.*

Closing Prayer

LEADER: God, our Father and giver of peace,
you sent us Jesus, your Son,
to show us how to live in peace
with you and with one another.
Send the Holy Spirit
to help us live as peacemakers.
We ask this through Jesus Christ our Lord.

ALL: Amen.

LEADER: The Lord frees us from our sins.
Live in peace.

ALL: Thanks be to God.

Opening Ritual

Objective
Experience the ritual action of sharing a peace greeting and reflect on its meaning.

Celebrate
Celebrate the Ritual
Lead the young people in the celebration of the opening ritual, which is found on page 190.

Reflect
Guide the young people in a reflection on their experience of the opening ritual. Invite them to talk about what it was like for them to share a peace greeting with one another.

Discover
Facilitate the young people's connection of the ritual experience of sharing peace with their daily lives. Ask the young people to describe some of the ways that they share peace with others each day.

Apply
Integrate
- Explain that when we live as peacemakers, we are living as children of God. As Catholics we are called to share the peace of Christ with one another.

- Explain that hospitality and peace are closely connected. Rooted in the faith belief that all people are children of God, practicing hospitality gives expression to our commitment to welcome others as God welcomes us. Throughout the Old Testament the Israelites welcomed guests—even unknown strangers—with hospitality, giving expression to their commitment to live the Covenant.

The Gift of Peace
(Scripture)

Objective
Tell the gospel story about the gift Jesus gave his disciples on the night before he died.

Teach
Connect
Recall with the young people their experience of the opening ritual of sharing a peace greeting.

Discover
- Distribute the handout "We Are Peacemakers." Ask the young people to describe what is meant by the word *peace*. Explain the rich meaning of the word *peace* found in the Bible by presenting the section "Bible Background." Use the "Think About It" question to summarize the discussion.
- Expand the discussion of peace by explaining that *shalom,* or God's gift of peace, will come about when all creation is reconciled in Christ and we live in communion with God and one another. Celebrating the sacrament of Reconciliation helps the Church continue this work of reestablishing *shalom*.
- Read the "Faith Focus" question aloud. Ask the young people to discover the answer as they listen to the Bible story.
- Invite a volunteer to proclaim the gospel story "The Gift of Peace," John 14:15–27 and John 20:21.

Reflect
Share the context of this Bible story with the young people. (John 14:15–27 took place at the Last Supper. John 20:21 took place after the Resurrection.) Have them imagine that they are with the disciples. Reflect on what hearing the words "I give you the gift of my peace" and "Peace be with you" must have meant to the disciples. If journal writing is part of your process, have the young people record their reflections in their journals.

Apply

Integrate

- Present and discuss the section "Understanding the Word of God."
- Have the young people work in small groups to discuss the "Think About It" questions.
- Discuss with the entire group ways that they can share Jesus' gift of peace with another group.

At Home

Encourage the young people to share what they have learned with their families.

LESSON PLAN

Blessed Are the Peacemakers
(Doctrine/Liturgy)

Objective

Explain that receiving and sharing Jesus' gift of peace is one of the effects of Reconciliation.

Teach

Connect

Recall the Bible story about Jesus sharing the gift of peace with his disciples. Invite volunteers to name people whom they know, or know of, who are peacemakers.

Discover

- Distribute the handout "Blessed Are the Peacemakers." Read aloud the "Faith Focus" question and have the young people discover the answer as you present the material on the handout.
- Present the section "Peacemakers." Emphasize that when we live as peacemakers, we are showing our love for Jesus.
- Continue by presenting the section "Sacrament of Peace." Make the connection between being a peacemaker and the sacrament of Reconciliation.
- Emphasize that celebrating Reconciliation calls us

to be living signs of the kingdom of God where we will all live in peace with God, Jesus, Mary, and the saints forever.

- Invite the young people to discuss the "Think About It" questions from both sections in small groups.

Reflect

Read aloud the opening paragraph and the Scripture quote based on Matthew 5:9. Ask and discuss: Why do you think Jesus called peacemakers blessed? If journal writing is part of your process, have the young people write their responses to the question in their journals.

Apply

Integrate

- Present "What We See and Hear." Explain that the Scripture quote from Matthew 5:9 is one of the Beatitudes. The Gospel according to Matthew presents a summary of Jesus' teaching in the Sermon on the Mount. The Beatitudes, which are part of the Sermon on the Mount (see Matthew 5:3–12), are sayings or teachings of Jesus that describe both the qualities and actions of people blessed by God. The word *beatitude* means "blessing" or "happiness." The Beatitudes are like signposts that help us find and share the happiness that God wants all his children to share. In each of the Beatitudes, Jesus describes one action that leads to the happiness God wants for all people. Each of the Beatitudes describes one way we can truly live the Great Commandment.

- Invite the young people to create a peacemaking poster. Provide various art materials and have them create a poster that will remind them to live as peacemakers.

At Home

Encourage the young people to share what they have learned with their families.

© RCL · Resources for Christian Living®

LESSON PLAN

What Difference Does This Make in My Life?/ Together as a Family

Objective
Decide to put our faith into action and make a difference.

Connect

Summarize

Recall the Beatitude "Blessed are the peacemakers. They are children of God." Then summarize ways we show we are peacemakers by presenting the first paragraph of the handout "What Difference Does This Make in My Life?"

Respond

Discover

- Have the young people look at the first activity on the "What Difference Does This Make in My Life?" handout. After a discussion of people who are peacemakers, have everyone complete the first activity.
- Invite the young people to pray to the Holy Spirit. After a few seconds, ask them to complete the second activity.

Choose

- Explain the faith decision activity. Invite everyone to quietly read it and think about how they might complete the faith decision activity.
- Extend the faith decision activity by brainstorming what the whole class can do together to show they are living as peacemakers.

Together as a Family

At Home

Distribute copies of the handout "Together as a Family." Invite the young people to share the page with their families.

Sending Forth Ritual

Play the recording of the instrumental version of an appropriate hymn from RCL's Reconciliation music CD. Then invite the young people to gather in the prayer area. Once they are settled, begin the ritual.

LEADER: God, our loving Father,
you give us new life
in your Son, Jesus, the Prince of Peace.
Help us live as peacemakers,
living signs of your love in the world.

ALL: Amen.

LEADER: Bow your heads and ask for God's blessing.
May God—the Father, the Son,
and the Holy Spirit—
help you to live as peacemakers.

ALL: Amen.

LEADER: *Invite the young people to come forward one at a time. Placing your hands on the top of each person's head, say,*
May the Holy Spirit fill your heart
with the gift of his peace.

ALL: Amen.

LEADER: *After all the young people have returned to their places ask God's blessing on the group, saying,*
May almighty God bless you,
the Father, and the Son, and the Holy Spirit.

ALL: Amen.

LEADER: Go in peace.

ALL: Thanks be to God.

CHAPTER 1 We Belong to God

Background Reflection

We are reborn to new life in Christ through the waters of Baptism and the gift of the Holy Spirit. God shares his life with us. We are joined to Christ and reconciled with God. We receive the gift of God's love, the Holy Spirit. The Holy Spirit helps us live as followers of Christ.

Jesus proclaimed God's love for all people. Using parables, Jesus taught about the unconditional love of God for all people. In one parable Jesus told the story about a good shepherd and his one lost sheep. The good shepherd goes to great lengths to find and care for the sheep. Like the love of a good shepherd for his sheep, God's love for us has no limits.

When children experience the caring of someone who loves them, they experience security and trust. They, in turn, enjoy and value caring for other people. In these experiences both of people truly caring for them and their own caring for other people, children can get a glimpse of the unique relationship God has entered into with them.

Sharing Together

What We Will Need

These are the items you will need for this lesson. Take the time to gather them in advance of meeting with your child:

- RCL's *Reconciliation* handouts for older children for chapter 1, "We Belong to God"
- Opening family ritual for chapter 1
- Large, clear bowl of water
- Bible

What We Will Learn

In your time together your family will deepen its understanding and living of the Church's faith. The faith theme of this lesson is: *We share new life in Christ through Baptism. Through Baptism God shares divine life with us. Baptism marks us as belonging to Jesus the Good Shepherd.*

What We Will Do

Follow these simple steps to join with your son or daughter in preparation for the celebration of the sacrament.

- **Preparation:** Read and reflect on the background reflection.

- **Step One: Celebrate the Ritual**
  —Celebrate the ritual "Blessing with Water."
  —Use the "Opening Ritual" section on the first page of the handout for chapter 1 to share what it was like to experience the family ritual.

- **Step Two: Share the Scripture Story**
  —Point out the "Faith Focus" question on the first page of the handout and together discover the answer as you listen to the Scripture story.
  —Using the Scripture section, "God Loves Us," read and talk about the "Bible Background." Then read and share your understanding of the Scripture story "The Parable of the Lost Sheep" (Luke 15:1-7). Read and discuss "Understanding the Word of God." Use the "Think About It" questions to guide your faith sharing.

- **Step Three: Discover the Faith of the Church**
  —Using the "Jesus, the Good Shepherd" page of the handout, point out the "Faith Focus" question. Read and discuss this page. Use the "Think About It" questions to guide your faith sharing.

- **Step Four: Make a Difference**
  —Choose to make a difference in your own lives and in the lives of others by living as followers of Jesus. Suggested activities are found on the "What Difference Does This Make in My Life?" page of the handout.
  —Enrich your time together. Read and discuss the "Together as a Family page of the handout. Choose one activity from "Sharing Together" that will help you live out your faith as a family.

- **Conclusion: Closing Prayer**
  Conclude your time together with a family prayer of your own choosing.

© RCL • Resources for Christian Living®

We Follow Jesus

Background Reflection

Jesus teaches us to love God with our whole heart and to love our neighbor as we love ourselves. These are the two parts of the Great Commandment. As his followers, Jesus calls us to live the law of love spelled out in the Great Commandment.

We begin by living this law of love among our families, friends, coworkers, and neighbors. It is often these people, who are closest to us, who cause us to think about how we are living. As we grow in faith and love, we can reach out beyond those closest to us to share the love of God with others.

Reverence is one of the Gifts of the Holy Spirit. This gift shapes our attitude of respect not only for God but also for other people—and for all life. Help your child discover that all life, especially human life, is sacred. Nurture in your child the development of the gift of reverence. Guide them to love every person as a child of God. It is on this foundation that children can truly learn to love God with their whole heart and to love others as they love themselves.

Sharing Together

What We Will Need

These are the items you will need for this lesson. Take the time to gather them in advance of meeting with your child:

- RCL's *Reconciliation* handouts for older children for chapter 2, "We Follow Jesus"
- Opening family ritual for chapter 2
- Bible

What We Will Learn

In your time together your family will deepen your understanding and living of the Church's faith. The faith theme of this lesson is: *The Great Commandment is the summary and the heart of all of God's commandments.*

What We Will Do

Follow these simple steps to join with your son or daughter in preparation for the celebration of the sacrament.

- **Preparation:** Read and reflect on the background reflection.

- **Step One: Celebrate the Ritual**
  —Celebrate the ritual "Reverence for the Word of God."
  —Use the "Opening Ritual section on the first page of the handout for chapter 2 to share what it was like to experience the family ritual.

- **Step Two: Share the Scripture Story**
  —Point out the "Faith Focus" question on the first page of the handout and together discover the answer as you listen to the Scripture story.
  —Using the Scripture section, "The Great Commandment," read and talk about the "Bible Background." Then read and share your understanding of the Scripture story "The Great Commandment" (Matthew 22:34–40). Read and discuss "Understanding the Word of God." Use the "Think About It" questions to guide your faith sharing.

- **Step Three: Discover the Faith of the Church**
  —Using the "Living a Holy Life" page of the handout, point out the "Faith Focus" question. Read and discuss this page. Use the "Think About It" questions to guide your faith sharing.

- **Step Four: Make a Difference**
  —Choose to make a difference in your own lives and in the lives of others by living as followers of Jesus. Suggested activities are found on the "What Difference Does This Make in My Life?" page of the handout.
  —Enrich your time together. Read and discuss the "Together as a Family" page of the handout. Choose one activity from "Sharing Together" that will help you live out your faith as a family.

- **Conclusion: Closing Prayer**
  Conclude your time together with a family prayer of your own choosing.

CHAPTER 3 We Listen to the Holy Spirit

Background Reflection

God has given us the special gifts of free will and conscience. By giving us these gifts God has given us the ability and the choice to love him. The choice to grow closer to God or away from God is ours to make. We can choose to turn toward God and respond to his love, or we can turn away from God and his love.

Our choice of God's love is reflected in the many good choices we make each day. Making good choices is not always easy. Fortunately we have a conscience that helps us make good choices by guiding us in knowing right from wrong. Conscience, like the muscles in our body, can be strengthened or allowed to grow weak.

A good conscience is one that is well formed and strengthened by prayer and a knowledge of faith through the Church's teachings. A well-formed conscience strengthens our freedom to make good decisions. The more we train our conscience to know what is good and what is evil, the better we will be at making those good decisions that help us live as followers of Jesus.

Sharing Together

What We Will Need

These are the items you will need for this lesson. Take the time to gather them in advance of meeting with your child.

- RCL's *Reconciliation* handouts for older children for chapter 3, "We Listen to the Holy Spirit"
- Opening family ritual for chapter 3
- Your child's baptismal candle or a large white candle
- Bible

What We Will Learn

In your time together your family will deepen your understanding and living of the Church's faith. The faith theme of this lesson is: *The Holy Spirit helps us make good decisions and put them into action.*

What We Will Do

Follow these simple steps to join with your son or daughter in preparation for the celebration of the sacrament.

- **Preparation:** Read and reflect on the background reflection.

- **Step One: Celebrate the Ritual**
  —Celebrate the ritual "Jesus, Light of the World."
  —Use the "Opening Ritual" section on the first page of the Handout for chapter 3 to share what it was like to experience the family ritual.

- **Step Two: Share the Scripture Story**
  —Point out the "Faith Focus" question on the first page of the handout and together discover the answer as you listen to the Scripture Story.
  —Using Scripture section, "The Good Samaritan," read and talk about the "Bible Background." Then read and share your understanding of the Scripture story " "The Good Samaritan" (Luke 10: 29–37). Read and discuss "Understanding the Word of God". Use the "Think About It" questions to guide your sharing.

- **Step Three: Discover the Faith of the Church**
  —Using the "We Make Good Decisions" page of the handout, point out the "Faith Focus" question. Read and discuss this page. Use the "Think About It" questions to guide your faith sharing.

- **Step Four: Make a Difference**
  —Choose to make a difference in your own lives and in the lives of other people by living as followers of Jesus. Suggested activities are found on the "What Difference Does This Make in My Life?" page of the handout.
  —Enrich your time together. Read and discuss the "Together as a Family" page of the handout. Choose one activity from "Sharing Together" that will help you live your faith as a family.

- **Conclusion: Closing Prayer**
  Conclude your time together with a family prayer of your own choosing.

We Are Sorry

Background Reflection

Jesus' work among us was a work of reconciliation and healing. When he walked among us, Jesus forgave sins and restored the health of numerous people whom he met. This healing now stretches out through the ministry of the Church, the Body of Christ, to all who call upon Jesus.

We receive the forgiveness of Christ through the sacrament of Reconciliation when we are truly sorry for our sins, confess our sins to a priest, accept and do a penance, and are absolved from our sins. The healing forgiveness of God restores us to spiritual health.

Praying the Our Father reminds us of the forgiving love of God and our call, as children of God, to share that forgiving love with other people. We show our joy and gratitude for God's forgiveness by forgiving others as Jesus taught us.

Sharing Together

What We Will Need

These are the items you will need for this lesson. Take the time to gather them in advance of meeting with your child.

- RCL's *Reconciliation* handouts for older children for chapter 4, "We Are Sorry"
- Opening family ritual for chapter 4
- Bible

What We Will Learn

In your time together your family will deepen your understanding and living of the Church's faith. The faith theme of this lesson is: *The prayer of sorrow, or act of contrition, and penance express our decision and desire to heal the harm we have caused by our sin and to be reconciled with God and the Church.*

What We Will Do

Follow these simple steps to join with your son or daughter in preparation for the celebration of the sacrament.

- **Preparation:** Read and reflect on the background reflection.
- **Step One: Celebrate the Ritual**
  —Celebrate the ritual "Praying the Our Father."
  —Use the "Opening Ritual" section of the first page of the handout for chapter 4 to share what it was like to experience the family ritual.
- **Step Two: Share the Scripture Story**
  —Point out the "Faith Focus" question on the first page of the handout and together discover the answer as you listen to the Scripture story.
  — Using the Scripture section, "Zacchaeus," read and talk about the "Bible Background." Then read and share your understanding of the Scripture story "Zacchaeus" (Luke 19: 1–10). Read and discuss "Understanding the Word of God." Use the "Think About It" questions to guide your sharing.
- **Step Three: Discover the Faith of the Church**
  —Using the "We Tell God We Are Sorry" page of the handout, point out the Faith Focus" question. Read and discuss this page. Use the "Think About It" questions to guide your sharing.
- **Step Four: Make a Difference**
  —Choose to make a difference in your own lives and in the lives of other People by living as followers of Jesus. Suggested activities are found on the "What Difference Does This Make in My Life?" page of the handout.
  —Enrich your time together. Read and discuss the "Together as a Family" handout. Choose one activity from "Sharing Together" that will help you live your faith as a family.
- **Conclusion: Closing Prayer**
  Conclude your time together with a family prayer of your own choosing.

5 We Are Forgiven

Background Reflection

One of the most touching parts of the parable of the forgiving father, or the parable of the prodigal son, is the son's return home and his being embraced by his father. The son's heart is filled with sorrow for having sinned against his father. The father, knowing and feeling his son's sorrow, embraces his son and welcomes him home—unconditionally—with a heart filled with joy.

Help your child understand that God always forgives us when we reach out to him in true sorrow for our sins, just as the son reached out to his father in the parable of the prodigal son.

In the ritual for this chapter you will experience the ritual action of laying on of hands. This gesture has a variety of meanings. During the sacrament of Reconciliation the priest lays hands on our head or over our head as he prays the prayer of absolution. This gesture reminds us that the work of forgiveness is the work of the Holy Spirit.

Sharing Together

What We Will Need

These are the items you will need for this lesson. Take the time to gather them in advance of meeting with your child.

- RCL's *Reconciliation* handouts for older children for chapter 5, "We Are Forgiven"
- Opening family ritual for chapter 5
- Bible

What We Will Learn

In your time together your family will deepen your understanding and living of the Church's faith. The faith theme of this lesson is: *In the sacrament of Reconciliation God forgives our sins through the ministry of bishops and priests.*

What We Will Do

Follow these simple steps to join with your son or daughter in preparation for the celebration of the sacrament.

- **Preparation:** Read and reflect on the background reflection.

- **Step One: Celebrate the Ritual**
  —Celebrate the ritual "Laying On of Hands"
  —Use the "Opening Ritual" section on the first page of the handout for chapter 5 to share what is was like to experience the family ritual.

- **Step Two: Share the Scripture Story**
  —Point out the "Faith Focus" question and together discover the answer as you listen to the Scripture story.
  —Using the Scripture page, "The Forgiving Father," read and talk about the "Bible Background." Then read and share your understanding of the Scripture story "The Forgiving Father" (Luke 15:11–32). Read and discuss the section "Understanding the Word of God." Use the "Think About It" questions to guide your sharing.

- **Step Three: Discover the Faith of the Church**
  —Using "The Gift of Forgiveness" page of the handout, point out the "Faith Focus" question. Read and discuss this handout. Use the "Think About It" questions to guide your sharing.

- **Step Four: Make a Difference**
  —Choose to make a difference in your own lives and in the lives of other people by living as followers of Jesus. Suggested activities are found on the "What Difference Does This Make in My Life?" handout.
  —Enrich your time together. Read and discuss the "Together as a Family" page of the handout. Choose one activity from "Sharing Together" that will help you live your faith as a family.

- **Conclusion: Closing Prayer**
  Conclude your time together with a family prayer of your own choosing.

We Are Peacemakers

Background Reflection

Jesus taught that children of God are peacemakers. Living as peacemakers is a responsibility that is not always easy to fulfill. At Baptism, we are anointed to be messengers of Jesus, the Prince of Peace. At Eucharist we are nourished to be messengers of peace through loving and serving God and one another.

Reconciliation also makes us sharers in God's gift of peace. We are freed from our sins and reconciled with God and with one another. We are sent forth to forgive and reconcile as God has forgiven and reconciled us to himself and to the church community.

We have been sent by Jesus, the Prince of Peace, to be messengers and agents of peace—not violence. What a difference it makes when we live as peacemakers. What a difference it makes, when we face a conflict or violence, to step back and control our impulse to get even.

Sharing Together

What We Will Need

These are the items you will need for this lesson. Take the time to gather them in advance of meeting with your child.

- RCL's *Reconciliation* handouts for older children for chapter 6, "We Are Peacemakers"
- Opening family ritual for chapter 6
- Bible

What We Will Learn

In your time together your family will deepen your understanding and living of the Church's faith. The faith theme of this lesson is: *The sacrament of Reconciliation makes us sharers in God's gift of peace and renews our calling to share that peace with others.*

What We Will Do

Follow these simple steps to join with your son or daughter in preparation for the celebration of the sacrament.

- **Preparation:** Read and reflect on the background reflection.

- **Step One: Celebrate the Ritual**
  —Celebrate the ritual "Sharing a Sign of Peace."
  —Use the "Opening Ritual" section of the first page of the handout for chapter 6 to share what it was like to experience the family ritual.

- **Step Two: Share the Scripture Story**
  —Point out the "Faith Focus" question on the first page of the handout and together discover the answer as you listen to the Scripture story.
  —Using the Scripture page, "The Gift of Peace," read and talk about the "Bible Background." Then read and share your understanding of the Scripture story "The Gift of Peace" (John 14:15–27 and 20–21). Read and discuss the section "Understanding the Word of God." Use the "Think About It" questions to guide your sharing.

- **Step Three: Discover the Faith of the Church**
  —Using the "Blessed Are the Peacemakers" page of the handout, point out the "Faith Focus" question. Read and discuss this handout. Use the "Think About It" questions to guide your sharing.

- **Step Four: Make a Difference**
  —Choose to make a difference in your own lives and in the lives of other people by living as followers of Jesus. Suggested activities are found on the "What Difference Does This Make in My Life?" handout.
  —Enrich your time together. Read and discuss the "Together as a Family" handout. Choose one activity from "Sharing Together" that will help you live your faith as a family.

- **Conclusion: Closing Prayer**
  Conclude your time together with a family prayer of your own choosing.